G000254716

UNDERSTANDING ANCIENT EGYPT

EILEEN GOULDING

Published by GOGO Publishing Ltd

© Eileen Goulding 2014

WWW.GOGO.PUB

9 780993 115202 >

ISBN 978-0-9931152-0-2

To Patricia & Graham,
lovely meeting
you. Very best
wishes,

Eileen xx

Contents

PREFACE

Most people have some knowledge about Ancient Egypt from books and documentaries, or have visited the ancient sites with knowledgeable guides. They will have been bombarded by a mass of information about gods, mummies, the pyramids, Tutankhamun and the tombs in the Valley of the Kings, all without structure or context, making it very difficult to make any sense of Egypt's ancient culture. This book aims to give the reader a frame of reference that will give accurate and interesting information, enabling them to gain a clear understanding of its people and their customs. It will correct many of the misconceptions they may have about the culture and development of Ancient Egypt and give them a real understanding of what it was like to live in the Land of the Pharaohs during their 3,000 years of power, whether as a king, a queen or a commoner.

Most books on Ancient Egypt are either simplistic 'Introductions' which mention a few aspects of their religion and culture, or they give in-depth analysis of one subject such as temples or pyramids – either way, the reader still ends up quite confused with no clear understanding of how it all worked together. This book is for people who are genuinely interested in the character of the Ancient Egyptians but whose lives leave them little time to study – people like me a few years ago. I was always interested in the subject but had never found the time to study it in depth and never found a one-volume book that gave me sufficient information on all topics. This book aims to address that problem and give its readers an understanding of all the different aspects of culture that made up this ancient society in one 'easy read'.

It is impossible to make sense of Ancient Egyptian civilisation without a clear understanding of their most important myths and how they related to normal, everyday life. There is a realisation today that myths are not childish stories but are part of the fabric of all human life, moulding beliefs and justifying behaviour. In ancient times man struggled to make sense of his world, and gods and their relationship with mankind became the myths which answered his questions about the natural environment, history and destiny. Every aspect of life for the Ancient Egyptians was linked to their belief system and governed what they did.

This book will tell you about their most important myths, prominent gods, powerful pharaohs and influential queens. You will learn about their very skilled tradesmen, what they built and most importantly, understand why. You will discover what they believed in, what magic and medicine they practiced and how they celebrated. It will also introduce you to their sacred hieroglyphic script.

This book will give the reader a clear understanding of what made an Ancient Egyptian 'tick', what was real to him and how all the parts of his life fitted together. It will give most readers as much information as they would wish for but may prompt others to study Egyptology in greater depth.

Of course, no one completes a project like this without some help. My husband Graham has supported me with kindness and enthusiasm, offering constructive comments on the text, and raising thoughtful and provocative questions. He has also created the maps and been my proof-reader, chief editor and photographer – thank you!

For Sofia, Leo, Isabella and Amelie

1 TIMELINE

When we refer to 'Ancient Egypt', we mean the time period starting around 3100 BC when the Early Dynastic period was founded by the Pharaoh Narmer. Scenes on artefacts dated to that time, such as the Narmer Palette and the Scorpion Macehead, suggest that warfare played an important role when he forged the early state of Egypt. He united the kingdoms of Upper and Lower Egypt into one political, cultural and economic domain, giving them a sense of common identity and purpose.

The period ends in 332 BC when the Greek general Alexander the Great invaded Egypt and founded the Grecian dynasty ruled by the Ptolemaics. The death in 30 BC of the Ptolemaic queen, Cleopatra VII Philopator, heralded the beginning of the Roman period and the demise of a great civilisation; Egypt became just a province of Rome and of subsequent invaders.

Between theses dates there are thirty dynasties based on a chronological system introduced in the early third century BC by the Egyptian historian and priest Manetho in his history of Egypt (the *Aegyptiaca*), with the later addition of a thirty-first dynasty. In ancient times, dates were recorded in relation to the length of reign of the pharaoh (regnal years) e.g. *Year 16*

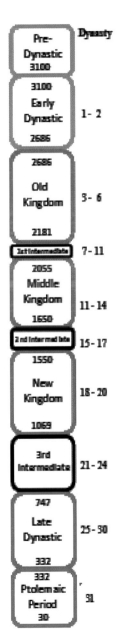

Rameses III. Based on Manetho's chronological system, this year in modern terms is 1168 BC. Further information on each sovereign's length of reign comes from pharaonic king lists such as the Turin Royal Canon, which is dated to the reign of Rameses II (1279-1213 BC). It takes its name from the Museo Egizio di Turin where it is housed. In this, the most complete of king lists, the groups of rulers tend to be treated as if they reigned one after the other. However, it is known that some of them (particularly from the 13th to 17th Dynasties) had overlapping periods when different kings simultaneously controlled separate parts of the country.

Each dynasty lasted one hundred years on average, a similar timespan to the various royal houses of Europe since the 1st century AD. The distinction between one dynasty and the next appears to have been in royal kinship and/or the location of the capital. Each dynasty consisted of groups of rulers with a shared kinship; when the ruling group changed it heralded the beginning of a new dynasty and sometimes the centralisation of power to a different area and city. The 'Kingdoms' were generally times of relative peace and prosperity when the country was united under one ruler, and the 'Intermediate' periods were times of uncertainty, poor governance and internal strife.

New evidence of kings and their reigns is being discovered regularly, which improves our knowledge but changes the chronology we have previously accepted as being correct. A recent discovery is that of a previously unknown king, Woseribre Senebkay, whose remains were found in a tomb south of Abydos, dated to the Second Intermediate Period (1650-1550 BC); his name will now be included in an amended chronological King List. Since our information about reigns is incomplete, all dates detailed here are those currently accepted by most Egyptologists but must be regarded as approximate.

2   EGYPT AND ITS PEOPLE

THE COUNTRY

Desert covered more than 90% of Ancient Egypt and was known as *deshret* or the 'Red Land' supporting only very small settlements in oases and wadis. The single most important geographical feature was the Nile River, the source of the wealth and prosperity that the Ancient Egyptians enjoyed. It is the longest river in the world, stretching from East Africa to the Mediterranean for over 6,800 km. It flows from south to north, hence the south of Egypt is called Upper Egypt since it is nearer to the mountainous source of the Nile, and the north is Lower Egypt. From earliest times the Nile was swollen by the summer rains in Ethiopia and Sudan, and

Figure 1 Map of Ancient Egypt

flooded every year between June and September, an occurrence known as the inundation. It brought new layers of rich alluvial soil that were deposited on the flood plain of Egypt. The climate and water surge of the Nile determined three seasons of four months each; the inundation, known as *akhet,* when the land was flooded, *peret* which was the growing season and *shemu* when the crops were harvested. Without its life-giving waters and fertile flood

3

plain, it is highly unlikely that Egyptian civilisation would have developed as successfully as it did in the deserts of north-eastern Africa. The High Dam at Aswan, built in the 1960's, ended the annual inundation and the previously fertile soil is now enriched by fertigation, a sprayed mixture of fertiliser and water.

During the Predynastic era, the ancient city of Buto was vitally important. Its maritime location was 95 km east of Alexandria, its position making it an important city for international trade where different cultures could conduct business and assimilate. The country had abundant natural mineral resources including gold, copper, amethyst and turquoise as well as building materials such as granite and limestone. The constant commercial traffic from neighbouring countries brought in suitable timber for boat building, together with a wonderful array of luxury items such as spices, silver, lapis lazuli, ebony and ivory, which the Egyptians traded against their own surplus resources.

The reunification of Egypt under Ahmose after the Second Intermediate Period, heralded a time of stability and great wealth. Large tracts of Nubia had been assimilated under Egyptian rule during the 17th Dynasty, and remained so for almost 500 years. Its enormous mineral resources, especially in gold, laid the foundation for Egypt's commercial success. During that period, the New Kingdom, Egypt was a particularly powerful, influential and wealthy country, becoming the major commercial power in the ancient world.

Cairo is the capital today but the neighbouring site of Memphis, some 24 km south of modern Cairo, was the capital city of the northern region (Lower Egypt) for most of the pharaonic period. It was the administrative capital during the Early Dynastic Period and the Old Kingdom and is said to have been founded by the 1st

Dynasty ruler, Narmer (also known as Menes). In later years, after Thebes was made the centre for religious worship and administration, Memphis continued to be regarded as the northern capital. The remains of this important city today lie beneath a thick layer of alluvium deposits, much of it below the water table which is steadily rising due to modern irrigation methods. Tombs of its rulers were located to the west of the city with Saqqara being the largest and nearest section of the necropolis (see Chapter 9 Pyramids).

The ancient southern (Upper Egypt) city of Thebes is where modern Luxor stands today. It was the principle city of the southern region, known at that time as Waset (the Greeks renamed it Thebes). It was a small town during the Old Kingdom but gradually developed in size and importance. In the 12th Dynasty Egypt's rulers established Thebes as their capital city, made the sun god Amun their local deity and built a temple complex at Karnak in his honour. The New Kingdom was the most important period in Theban history when successive rulers made it the centre of administration and religious focus and began to enlarge and elaborate the temple complex. It remains the largest and best-preserved temple complex of the New Kingdom, covering over a hundred hectares, and is an important source of written texts concerning the religious and political activities of pharaonic Egypt. Opposite Thebes, on the west bank of the Nile, the Valley of the Kings became the established burial ground for pharaohs with queens and high officials buried nearby on the hill slopes. In the Ramesside Period (late New Kingdom), the royal palace and central administration transferred to the Delta but Thebes retained much of its religious and political significance.

SYMBOLISM OF UPPER AND LOWER EGYPT

The pharaoh Narmer united the two main regions of Egypt and thereafter the pharaoh's titles included 'King of Upper Egypt' and 'King of Lower Egypt', proclaiming this achievement. During the Intermediate Periods, each region had its own king who held only one of those titles. Each region had its own specific deity and symbols that were used in crowns, jewellery, furniture and reliefs. Upper Egypt was protected by the vulture goddess Nekhbet and the pharaoh wore a conical white crown *(hedjet)*, sometimes referred to as the White Nefer. The lotus flower was an emblem of Upper Egypt symbolising rebirth and its design was often incorporated into temple pillars.

Lower Egypt had the protection of the cobra deity Wadjyt, and the king wore a tall 'chair-shaped' red crown (*deshret*) with a protruding coil. Its heraldic emblem was the papyrus plant that grew in profusion in the northern Delta marshes. Like the lotus flower, it was also linked to the creation myths and its design was used for the columns of hypostyle halls.

Hedjet | Deshret | Pschent

As a ruler of the two lands the pharaoh's crown was a combination of the white and red crowns *(pschent)* Figure 2 Three Crowns of Egypt and included the protective images of the vulture and cobra deities who are often referred to as the 'two ladies' in royal titles.

THE PEOPLE

It is believed that the earliest humans migrated from East Africa and arrived in Israel as early as 1.8 million years ago. There is therefore, reason to believe that some of them settled in the Nile Valley as they passed through the country. However, with the exception of hand axes and similar chopping tools, evidence of human occupation of Egypt is scarce prior to the Middle Palaeolithic Era (70-100,000 years ago). Although the Nile brought richness and life to the Nile valley, it also brought about the erosion of older archaeological deposits leaving few remains from the earliest occupation of the country.

The earliest Neolithic cultures were cattle herders based in the Western Desert, but most sites were short-term camps of hunter-gatherers that were seasonally abandoned. The earliest Egyptian settlers were

Figure 3 Farming in Ancient Egypt

farmers who established homes along the banks of the Nile *c*.5000 BC in Upper Egypt in the region of el-Badari, and worked together in small communities. Evidence suggests that the economy of the culture was based on agriculture and husbandry. They still hunted wild animals which were their main source of meat but they also domesticated cattle, pigs, sheep and goats. One of the earliest Neolithic sites in Egypt is a large village called Merimda in the western Delta. The presence of polished stone axes, fishhooks and well-made arrowheads indicates that the villagers hunted for their food, but they also seem to have grown grain; archaeological evidence suggests that a variety of domesticated barley, apparently brought from western Asia, was stored in large jars and baskets near their reed and clay houses.

The farmers cultivated a wide variety of crops including emmer wheat and barley, lettuce, onions, lentils, figs and pomegranates. They fashioned the irrigation canals, basins and terracing which held the floodwater over the fields until all the rich, black silt had been deposited. This fertile black soil was known as *kemet* or the 'Black Land'.

The rich soil ensured abundant crops to feed the whole population, with frequently enough left over to put into storage for less bountiful years and for export to other countries. The correct level of inundation was vital since a lighter inundation than normal would cause famine, and too much flood water would be as great a calamity, washing away much of the infrastructure built on the flood plain.

The natural wealth of Egypt coupled with its geographical position made it the centre of international trade in the area. This enabled the assimilation

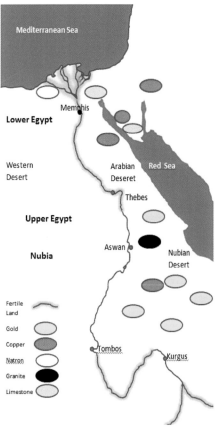

Figure 4 Natural resources map

8

of different races resulting in a socially complex society. Its multi-cultural people eventually produced a civilisation that was characterised by its own beliefs and myths, the basis of the religion, culture and unified land they strove to maintain for over 3,000 years.

GOVERNMENT

The Egyptian structure of government was hierarchical and formal, with the king at its head and the central source of authority, his power base filled by his supporters. The government excelled in the process of social and economic control of the population. The king's officials were empowered by attendance at the royal court, and bore the royal seal when they travelled the country on official business. The courtiers waited on the king, administered law and order throughout the land and sometimes served as military officers and priests if events so demanded. The government's most powerful official was the vizier (chief minister) who represented the king in most areas of government (excluding the military and religion). During the Intermediate Periods, when there was a rapid succession of rulers, it seems that the viziers provided the essential stability that stopped the administration from completely breaking up.

The common factor that set all these men apart from the common people was the fact that they were literate; they could read, write and complete mathematical calculations, and thereby were able to control the functions of the administration. This centralised system enabled the organisation of labour for expeditions to foreign lands to trade, building projects throughout the country, and mining operations in the surrounding deserts.

The country was divided into forty-two provinces called nomes, twenty-two in Upper Egypt and twenty in Lower Egypt. Each province had a nomarch (governor) who retained a degree of independence but was answerable to the central government. Whenever the royal court was weakened through inept kingship, war or economic decline, power tended to be taken by the nomarchs, who sometimes ousted the pharaoh and declared themselves the new king, for instance during the Intermediate Periods.

The national administration was divided into three sections; the 'dynasty', internal administration and external affairs. The 'dynasty' dealt with relatives of the king who had to be looked after but held no political or economical power, probably because it was they who might pose a threat to the current king's rule. The internal administration itself had four centres of responsibility: royal appointed positions such as chancellor, chamberlain and chief steward, the military, the priesthood and civil (secular) officials. External affairs involved the control and administration of Egyptian colonies in Nubia and elsewhere, depending on the power base of Egypt at the time.

The administration of the government revolved around the collection of taxes based on the quantity and quality of the harvest; government scribes, some of the most important people in the administration, are often referred to as 'grain counters'. The harvest depended on the correct level of inundation and for that reason, in an attempt to predict the level of the annual flood, and therefore how bountiful or otherwise the harvest would be, measuring devices called nilometers were built along the Nile. They were usually located at major temples including those at Philae, Edfu and Kom Ombo. The height of the floodwater was recorded each year in order to prepare for famine or an excessive flood. The simplest of the nilometers consisted of a vertical column submerged into the river, with marked intervals indicating the depth of the water.

The best-known surviving example, rebuilt during Roman times, is on the island of Elephantine at Aswan. It is a much more complicated structure of steps leading down to the water table with height levels marked into the stone. Its position was particularly important since, for much of Ancient Egypt's history, it marked the country's southern border and was therefore the first place where the onset of the annual flood was detected.

Most of the agricultural land belonged to the king, or to the temples that were administered by the priesthood, who rented out parcels of land to tenant farmers. Central and provincial administrators collected rent and taxes based on a biennial census of agricultural produce. Scenes from the tombs of private individuals show that scribes measured the precise area of land under cultivation and the numbers of livestock held by each farmer. In this non-monetary society, the tax was paid in kind, usually grain that was then held in huge government and temple granaries, and livestock. Severe penalties were enforced on defaulting farmers, even when their harvest had failed, but some individuals and institutions seem to have benefitted from 'exemption decrees'.

During the Old Kingdom there was no permanent national army although the king would have had a small royal bodyguard. However, by the Middle Kingdom a large national army had been created, part based in permanent fortresses and garrisons in Nubia with a considerable military infrastructure administered by government scribes and bureaucrats. The military profession was well established by the New Kingdom and campaigns were launched into Western Asia, Libya and Nubia consisting of four or five large divisions, each of about five thousand professional and conscripted soldiers. Mercenaries and slaves, who were able to gain their freedom by serving in the army, were also employed to make up the necessary numbers in times of conflict. The military profession was so powerful during this period that some of its most significant men rose to the position of pharaoh e.g Horemheb (1323-1295 BC) and Rameses I (1295-1294 BC).

THE LEGAL SYSTEM

During the Late Period there was a legal code set down in eight books but there is no documentary evidence that laws were codified prior to that time. Egyptian law was based on the concept of *maat* (truth and justice) and the common sense view of right and wrong based on the social norms of the day. Our knowledge of their system is based on 'wisdom literature,' funerary texts and documents found in the village of Deir el-Medina.

The ultimate authority in legal matters was the pharaoh who delegated this duty to his vizier and other court officials. It is thought that they wore a *maat* pendant on a chain around their neck when carrying out their legal duties. Serious cases would have been dealt with by the court officials but minor cases were heard locally, the 'judges' deciding on the guilt of the accused and meting out punishment where appropriate. Records of cases, the verdicts and punishments, were automatically archived either in the temple (serious cases), or in local libraries. This enabled them to issue similar punishments for similar offences based on precedent.

Villages such as Deir el-Medina had a local court comprising of a council of elders (men and women), a captain of one of the workers gangs, the chief police officer and a scribe from the vizier's office. They ruled on matters such as theft and non-payment of debts, referring more serious cases to the vizier himself. Evidence was given under oath, the council sometimes questioned the litigants, and witnesses were called to corroborate certain points. Texts indicate that where one party promised to compensate another by a certain date, the punishment if they failed to do so was a beating and a penalty of double payment. In the case of the washerwoman Bak-en-werl she swore, '*if I do not hand over these 4 skeins of yarn to the workman Ptah-shed on the third month of winter, day 10, I will get 100 blows and they will be reckoned against me double.*'

If a man deserted from military service or failed to complete the corveé labour demanded by the state, his family could suffer imprisonment. Similarly, if a person was exiled, his family was automatically outlawed along with them.

EDUCATION
The elite members of Egyptian society were taught reading, writing and mathematics, which provided them with the skills necessary to run the economic and administrative aspects of government. Learning seems to have been done by rote, with students copying out exercises and committing long passages of text to memory. Mathematics lessons addressed quite sophisticated problems that were broken down into simple small calculations, and were taught using numerous examples. Male children of the elite were taught in scribal schools, often connected to the palace or main temple, but there is no record of females being given the same privilege.

Figure 5 Scribe

However, the majority of the people were not given any formal education at all and were illiterate. The boys usually trained in practical trades and crafts, taught from one generation to another, often serving apprenticeships under their fathers. A son would eventually take over his father's trade and be the main provider for the family. There is little evidence to suggest that girls took any formal training or education although daughters naturally learned domestic skills such as cooking and weaving from their mothers. It is evident that a small proportion of women were literate; surviving letters to and from women in the village of Deir el-Medina may have been written personally by them. It seems quite feasible since it is believed that the literacy rate in this village of elite workmen was 40% compared to the country in general which was only 4%. Literary evidence suggests that the boys here practiced their writing on ostraca in scribal schools prior to taking up work in the Valley of the Kings. Although they did not attend school, girls may have learnt the skill from their male relatives. Another theory is that the letters were written and read by male scribes on behalf of their female patrons.

RELIGION

The state religion of Ancient Egypt was concerned with maintaining 'divine order', one of the chief responsibilities of the pharaoh. He had to ensure that life in his realm was conducted with *maat,* which represented truth, justice and harmony. Therefore, it was necessary that religion permeated all aspects of life, embedded in society rather than being a separate category. They took a holistic view of religion and the universe, incorporating apparently contradictory myths with prayers to the gods, magic, medicine and science, all with the same aim; to maintain harmony and suppress evil. The temples and the attendant priesthood were the focus of this aim. Each day they attended to the gods' daily needs for food and fresh clothing, made offerings to him and therefore kept the forces of evil and chaos at bay.

There were many different deities throughout Egypt's ancient history and temple cults were established in different areas and cities. For example, Thebes was the cult centre of the sun god Amun from the 11th Dynasty onwards and Osiris had his main southern cult centre at Abydos, said to be the burial place of his head.

The priests cannot be viewed as similar to clergymen today; they were regarded as 'servants of god' but were not necessarily well versed in religious doctrine. Many of them worked part-time as priests for a few months each year and then went back to their regular secular professions. In theory, the pharaoh was the high priest of every cult but in practice his role was delegated to the chief priest of the temple; only they had the privilege of attending the god. The chief priest had great power and influence, his position giving him authority in what we today would regard as secular matters of state. The chief priest was supported by lower ranking priests who attended to festivals, minor rituals and the economic organisation of the temple institution. Some groups of priests had specialist knowledge; astronomers who classified and described celestial phenomena, astrologers who determined auspicious days, instructors who taught reading and writing, and 'lector priests' who recited the words of the god. The Greek historian Herodotus stated that the Egyptian priests were required to be circumcised, to be entirely clean-shaven without any body hair, and to wash twice during the day and twice during the night. There was no prohibition to marriage but they had to abstain from sexual intercourse during their months of office. They were not allowed to wear wool or leather and their sandals had to be made from papyrus. Cult singers with titles such as 'chantress of Amun', and musicians and dancers accompanied the priests during rituals, their role normally carried out by women of noble birth. The economic organisation of the temple involved ensuring that the labourers conducted their tasks correctly, the appropriate payments (taxes) were received from their estates, and that the requisite number of food offerings were brought in each day. The Egyptians believed that the gods consumed the essence of the food offerings, the physical substance was then eaten by the priests, other temple staff and their families.

Figure 6 Pylons at Khons Temple Karnak

The Egyptians regarded the temple as the house of a deity, or family of deities, where the process of the first great Creation was replicated. The essential component of a temple was the innermost shrine where an image of the god was kept (usually a larger than life-sized statue). The most important temples comprised of a complex of buildings and processional walkways through which the king and priests could gradually approach the cult image of the god. The processional walkways passed through large open courtyards and massive ceremonial gateways known as pylons, into hypostyle halls with gigantic columns supporting the roof. A pylon consisted of two tapering towers representing the two mountains of the horizon through which the sun rose. A bridge of masonry linked them and rituals to the sun god were carried out on top of the gateway. The pylon was the most visible part of the temple to the great mass of the population who were not allowed past the first courtyard. They were brightly decorated with paint and inlays, the scenes depicting themes of royal power such as the king smiting foreign enemies. Most temples had only one pylon but the temple of Amun at Karnak has ten.

Very few pre-New Kingdom temples have survived, largely because they were repeatedly built over and their original design obliterated. An example of an Upper Egyptian design from the New Kingdom is in the precinct at Karnak with its temples dedicated to Amun, his consort Mut and son Khons.

The Creation symbolism is demonstrated very well in the hypostyle hall in the temple of Amun. The hall is crowded with a forest of 134 giant columns representing papyrus plants growing out of the primeval mound, each 23 m in height. Beyond the hall, the roof of the temple becomes lower and the floor higher, the rooms gradually becoming smaller until the inner sanctuary is reached.

Figure 7 Hypostyle Hall Karnak

Private religion practised by the general population was very different from state religion. Although they worshipped the state gods who maintained harmony throughout the land, they also had their own local and favourite deities that they worshipped at home and in small local temples and chapels. On the outskirts of Deir el-Medina for instance, there is a large chapel dedicated to Hathor, cow-goddess of love and fertility. Excavation of the chapel led to the discovery of a statue of another female deity, the snake goddess Meretseger. The god Ptah, patron of craftsmen, was another popular and appropriate god for the artisans of Deir el-Medina. In their homes, images of Bes and Taweret, protective deities of women and

17

children, were displayed and painted on the walls. They not only worshipped gods but also mortals and deified kings. One of the most important religious centres of the village was the temple dedicated to Amenhotep I, a deified king, and his mother Ahmes-Nefertari who was the first royal woman to have the title 'God's Wife of Amun' bestowed upon her. Amenhotep I was regarded as patron of the village although it was his successor Thutmose I who actually established the original team of skilled workmen. The villagers worked in the local chapels and temples as priests, songstresses and dancers in their spare time, possibly enacting the same daily ceremonies that were carried out in the main temples.

The religion of Ancient Egypt had hundreds of deities, several myths which explained Creation, and numerous beliefs, rituals and practices which took them from birth to death and beyond.

3   MYTHS AND FUNERARY BELIEFS

Creation, Kingship and Resurrection

Our knowledge of the activities of gods in the mythology of Ancient Egypt, and their interaction with mankind, has in general been taken from the words of hymns and funerary texts. Enactments of rituals painted on the walls of temples and tombs and described in hieroglyphics, enable us to visualise their deities as the Egyptians did themselves. Several literary texts have also survived such as *The Tale of Horus and Seth*; together, they have enabled Egyptologists to reconstruct versions of a variety of myths that were the foundation of Ancient Egyptian religion.

The three main categories of myths can be labelled Creation, Kingship and Resurrection; here is an illustration of each of them.

CREATION

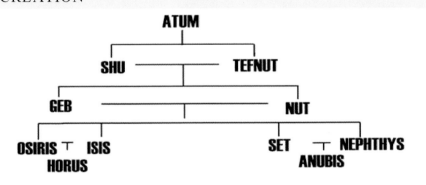

Figure 8 Family Tree of the god Atum

There were three main Egyptian creation myths, each named after the gods and cities where they originated: the Hermopolis Ogdoad (eight deities), the Heliopolis Ennead (nine deities) and the Memphis Theology (one deity, Ptah). The myths were all very

19

similar and complementary, involving gods who created the world and went on to create other gods and every living thing. As an example, this is the creation myth from the city of Heliopolis of a group of gods known as the Great Ennead of Heliopolis, whose relationships are first described in the *Pyramid Texts*.

The Ennead consisted of the creator sun god Atum and three generations of his descendants: his children Shu and Tefnut, his grandchildren Geb and Nut, and four great grandchildren Osiris, Isis, Set (or Seth) and Nepthys. The next generation included the falcon god Horus, son of Osiris and Isis, and Anubis the jackal god.

Figure 9 Atum

In the beginning, the world was covered in the lifeless waters of chaos. When the water gradually receded, the first thing to emerge was a pyramid-shaped mound of soil, called the *benben*. The flooding of the Nile River each year probably inspired this simple beginning; the receding floodwaters left fertile soil behind creating life from the previously lifeless waters. In recognition of this event at the beginning of time, the gilded capstone placed at the top of each pyramid or obelisk was called a *benbenet*. The burial tombs of the pharaohs, the *mastabas* and pyramids, represented the mound of creation where they believed their new eternal life would begin.

The first entity to rise from this primeval mound of earth was the sun god Atum, who was a self-made god, the source of all the elements and forces in the world. He created Shu the god of air and his sister Tefnut, goddess of moisture and fertility, through his own semen that was sneezed from his nose and spat from his mouth. Shu and Tefnut coupled and went on to produce Geb the god of earth and the sky goddess Nut, who defined the limits of the world. Shu is depicted as a man with his arms raised to support the sky, filling the space between the earth (Geb) and the star-filled sky (Nut). It was believed that Tefnut, goddess of moisture, purified the land each day with the morning dew.

Geb and Nut together created four children, who represented the forces of life: Osiris, god of fertility and regeneration; Isis, goddess of motherhood; Seth, the god of male sexuality and Nephthys, the goddess of female sexuality. The myth therefore represented the process by which all life was made possible. They were regarded as a group of nine gods but the eight descendants of Atum were regarded as lesser gods, since all things in the world were ultimately seen as an extension of the power of Atum.

The first five deities of the Ennead of Heliopolis, (Atum, Shu, Tefnut, Geb and Nut) explained the creation of the environment, albeit in a simplistic way, but the last four (Osiris, Isis, Seth and Nephthys) were the more important gods since they explained the laws of kingship and succession. Belief in those gods enabled everyone, royalty and commoners alike, to have trust and confidence in the rule of the pharaoh, allowing them to worship other minor gods who were more relevant to their everyday lives.

KINGSHIP

There are the two main myths relating to kingship:

THE ISIS AND OSIRIS MYTH

Before mortal man ruled the earth, the gods governed Egypt but filial jealousy provoked a battle for kingship. This is the Egyptian account of the battle for power:

The god Osiris taught mankind how to obey the laws of the gods, grow crops and make wine and was the most popular and loved of all the gods. His sister (now wife) Isis taught human wives how to make bread and beer, and encapsulated all the virtues of an Egyptian wife and mother. Their brother Seth was intensely jealous of Osiris' popularity and plotted to get rid of him so that he could take the throne for himself.

Seth built a box of priceless wood to Osiris' exact measurements, and then arranged a banquet. He declared to all present that whoever could fit inside the box could keep it. Many tried and failed but when Osiris lay down it was a perfect fit. Before Osiris could claim his prize, Seth closed the lid, locking him inside, and threw the box into the river Nile. It drifted away and Osiris eventually drowned.

After searching for a long time, Isis found the box containing the dead Osiris, but immediately fell into an exhausted sleep. Their brother Seth discovered her with the body and chopped it into fourteen pieces, scattering them throughout Egypt. Her tears when she discovered how her husband's body had been desecrated are said to be the cause of the first inundation.

Isis and her sister Nephthys searched the whole of Egypt and finally recovered thirteen of Osiris' body parts and built a tomb at each site; the only part missing was his penis which had been eaten by a fish. Isis put all thirteen body parts together and fashioned a penis out of clay. She then turned herself into a kite (bird), using her wings to breathe life back into her husband and became impregnated with their son Horus. That was the final act of Osiris in this world; Seth took over as ruler of Egypt and Osiris stayed in the realm of the dead where he remained forever as the god of the Underworld, judging the dead before they could pass on to the Afterlife.

THE HORUS AND SETH MYTH

His mother Isis raised Horus secretly but when he was old enough, he laid claim to his rightful place as heir to the throne, looking to avenge his father's murder. Seth refused to stand down and called for a tribunal of gods to decide who should be king.

Figure 10 Wedjat eye amulet

Over the next eighty years, various judgements were passed down from the tribunal, all in favour of Horus taking over as king, but Seth refused to accept their decision. There were many battles between Horus and Seth, including one when Horus lost his left eye, which represented the moon. Luckily, the goddess Hathor was able to save it, and Horus offered it to his father Osiris in the hope it would make him live again. The left eye of Horus therefore came to symbolise the general process of 'making whole' and healing and is

23

represented by the *wedjat*-eye. It was worn as a protective amulet and symbolised sacrifice, healing, and restoration.

The gods gave their final judgement that the throne of Egypt belonged to Horus. As a consolation prize, they made Seth, who was an outsider and the antithesis of his brother Osiris, the ruler of the deserts and the god of chaos and evil.

This myth confirmed two aspects of kingship; the act of succession whereby a son succeeded his father as king of Egypt and the importance of balance and order (Horus) over chaos (Seth). It also led to the belief that the pharaoh was Horus while he lived and ruled on earth and then became Osiris when he died and ruled the Underworld.

RESURRECTION

The belief system of the Ancient Egyptians pertaining to life and death was very complex, but it depended on the identification of the deceased with the murdered Osiris who was brought back to life by the efforts of Isis.

They believed that death was a short interruption in their life; they could live for eternity if they showed sufficient piety to the gods, preserved their body through mummification and took with them all the goods and equipment they would need in the next world. After death, they had to travel through the Underworld. Unlike modern ideas of the underworld that conjures up images of hell for all eternity, the Egyptians' Underworld was a transitional place of trials, tests and final judgement that would lead to the Afterlife. There are many conflicting descriptions of the Afterlife ranging from a heavenly, harmonious world free from hunger, poverty and disease, to another belief in the transformation of the deceased into stars.

The Egyptians believed that the essence of each individual was made up of six crucial elements, none of which could be neglected or could survive without the others; the physical body, his name, his shadow and three spirits, the *ka*, the *ba* and the *akh*. The process of preparation for burial, with all the accompanying rites and rituals, was therefore quite a balancing act to ensure all of the elements were sustained and protected from harm. Sufficient resources had to be dedicated to each element to guarantee a person's full enjoyment of the Afterlife. The body had to be preserved by mummification and provided with sustenance in the next life. They believed that this could be done by painting piles of food and drink on the walls of the tombs and writing about them in hieroglyphics. By naming them and representing them in pictures, they would 'magically' be fresh and wholesome and last for all eternity. Similarly, words and pictures representing the deceased would ensure he lived for ever.

On his death, the king was transformed into Osiris, but non-royal individuals believed they could re-enact the myth of Osiris' resurrection and would therefore achieve eternal life for themselves. Osiris was the most important god related to resurrection, but two other gods had a vital role in resurrection mythology, each with a crucial part to play in the deceased's journey to the Afterlife:

Khepri: a creator god represented by a scarab or dung beetle and associated with the sun and resurrection. The Egyptians had observed that with the dawn, the dung beetle came out of its hiding place and pushed a ball of dung; like a miracle, by sunset, tiny baby beetles emerged from the same ball. Although this does not actually represent its life-cycle, to them the dung beetle represented the passing of the sun through the day and then new birth. Khepri therefore became linked with the sun and new life (resurrection). The scarab form amulet was very popular and was produced in vast quantities from about the Middle Kingdom onwards.

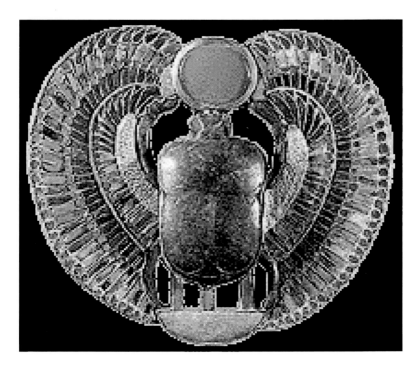

Figure 11 Winged Scarab

A variation of the scarab amulet was the Heart Scarab that was placed over the heart of the deceased within the mummy wrappings. On one side, it had the text from spell 30B from the *Book of the Dead*, which pleaded with the heart not to denounce the deceased during the Weighing of the Heart on judgement day:

'O my heart of my mother! ...Do not stand up as a witness against me, do not be opposed to me in the tribunal, do not be hostile to me in the presence of the Keeper of the Balance,... Do not tell lies about me in the presence of the god. It is indeed well that you should hear!'

Anubis: a jackal god, guardian of the deceased and god of embalming and mummification. He protected the deceased on his journey through the Underworld and is seen holding the deceased's hand on judgement day. He is also depicted holding the scales on which the heart was weighed to ensure they are balanced correctly.

The connection between a jackal and the deceased probably derived from the fact that in the Predynastic era corpses were not mummified and were usually buried in the desert sands where jackals would sometimes find them and dig up the bodies. Having the jackal as a protective god was to ward off the possibility that the deceased would be dug up, dismembered and eaten by the wild dogs of the wilderness.

Figure 12 Anubis

4   GODS AND GODDESSES

Ancient Egypt's Most Powerful Deities

Religion was fundamental to Ancient Egyptian society and, of course, gods are the foundation of religion. It is difficult sometimes to work out who was who, since the gods were often represented in both animal and human form; for instance, Thoth was depicted as a baboon and as a man with the head of the sacred ibis. Each had several names and could have overlapping roles, so Hathor and Isis were both regarded as the mother of Horus, and therefore the divine mother of the pharaoh. Here is a glimpse into their complex system of deities (see Chapter 2 for the foundation of their belief system), and some of their more powerful and popular gods and goddesses.

In general, they were separated into state and personal divinities. The state religion deities were presented in the temples, presided over by the pharaoh and the priesthood, and were most concerned with environmental issues such as the inundation, the complexities of the solar system, kingship succession and the pharaoh's chief role, maintaining harmony throughout the land. Ordinary people worshipped different gods and goddesses in their homes and were more concerned with their daily lives and the problems of fertility, childbirth and illness. Some deities were popular with kings and commoners alike; for instance, Hapy the god of the life-giving inundation, Isis (the mother of the falcon god Horus) who had general appeal as a 'mother', and Ptah a creator god who was worshipped as the god of craftsmen.

GODS

AMUN

There were many important sun gods throughout Ancient Egyptian history including Atum, Ra and Aten, but the sun god with the most influence on their religion and society, was Amun. His name means 'the hidden one' and he is usually depicted as a human male wearing a double-plumed crown, sometimes with the head of a ram, often in its full animal form. He was also combined with other powerful sun gods such as Ra (making him Amun-Ra). He was first mentioned in the 5th Dynasty and rose to his pre-eminent position by the Middle Kingdom

Figure 13 Amun

(*c.*2055 BC), most probably because he was the chosen local deity of the Theban pharaohs. He was regarded as 'the king of the gods' and by the time of the Ptolemaic period he was regarded as the Egyptian equivalent of the Greek god Zeus.

OSIRIS

Osiris was one of the earliest and most important gods, principally

associated with death, resurrection and fertility and was a key player in one of Egypt's greatest legends (see Chapter 2 The Myths). He is usually depicted as a mummified male whose hands project through the wrappings to hold the royal insignia of crook and flail. His flesh is normally shown as coloured green in allusion to new life (resurrection) but sometimes black to represent the fertile

Figure 14 Osiris

29

deposits of the Nile, or white like the mummy wrappings. Osiris was ruler of the Underworld, signified by his crown, known as the *atef*, which consists of the tall white crown of Upper Egypt flanked by two ostrich feathers. His best-known title was *wennefer*, meaning 'eternally good'. It was believed that the 'divine' pharaoh became Osiris when he died and passed into the Afterlife.

SETH

Seth was the brother of Osiris and was his opposite, being the evil god of chaos and confusion. He had a violent nature, instigating storms and bad weather. He was closely associated with the Red Lands of the desert and foreign countries, both of which were regarded with hostility by the Egyptians. He is portrayed as a man with squared ears and the long nose of an animal, which is reminiscent of an anteater but may have been a mythical creature. In full animal form, he had a canine body and erect forked tail but was also sometimes shown as a hippopotamus, pig or donkey. Despite his unsavoury character he was revered during the 2nd Dynasty and was venerated by the rulers of the 19th Dynasty for his strength in battle; two even took a derivation of his name (Sety) as their own. From *c.*800 BC, he was regarded as totally evil.

Figure 15 Seth

HORUS

He was the falcon-god, son of Osiris and the goddess Isis. He was

the god of the sky, the protector of the king and the embodiment of divine kingship; the pharaoh was regarded as the god Horus during his lifetime. He was usually depicted either as a hawk or as a man with the head of a hawk wearing the double crown of Upper and Lower Egypt. From the Late Period (*c.*747 BC) a new image of Horus, the *cippus*, became popular; it was a stele (slab of stone or

Figure 16 Horus wood) of Horus as a naked child standing on a crocodile and holding in his hands snakes, scorpions, lions or other animals. It was believed to provide healing power against the bites and stings of the creatures he held.

MIN

Fertility god and symbol of male potency, he was already being worshipped in the late Predynastic period (*c.*

3100 BC). He is depicted as a mummified male with a royal flail above his right arm that is raised in a smiting gesture; his left hand holds an erect phallus. As early as the 6th Dynasty he was linked with the cos lettuce, probably because its milky sap was seen to resemble semen. He served as the protector of Egyptian mining areas in the Eastern Desert and was also incorporated into the ceremonies

Figure 17 Min

surrounding the king, such as his coronation, designed to ensure the pharaoh's potency.

THOTH

This revered god of scribes was depicted in the form of two

animals; the baboon and a human male with the head of the sacred ibis. Thoth, originally a moon deity, was the god of wisdom, knowledge and writing, and was usually depicted holding a scribal palette and pen and engaged in some form of recording. He is shown attending all major scenes involving disputes between the gods, but most especially at the judgement of the dead, known as 'The Weighing of the Heart'. His consort was Maat, goddess of truth and justice.

Figure 18 Thoth

GODDESSES

ISIS

Isis was worshipped throughout Egypt but had her most significant cult centre at Philae near Aswan. She survived there as a goddess until the sixth century AD by which time the rest of Egypt had become Christianised. She was the devoted sister-wife of Osiris and

the mother of Horus, encapsulating all the virtues and qualities of a wife and mother. She was the symbolic mother of the pharaoh, as he himself was regarded as the living manifestation of Horus. In many scenes and statuettes, she is seen suckling the child Horus who is seated on her lap. She was closely

Figure 19 Isis

linked with the other 'mother' goddess Hathor and is often depicted with a headdress of a solar disc between two cow horns. In other depictions, she has long elegant wings that embrace the pharaoh, and in funerary scenes, she encloses the deceased within them.

MAAT

Figure 20 Maat

She was the goddess who personified truth, harmony and justice, and was usually depicted as a single feather or as a seated woman with outspread wings. Her headdress, which is always an ostrich feather, differentiates her from Isis.

She represented the divine order of the universe and her power regulated the movement of the stars, the seasons and the relationship between men and the gods. She was central to Egyptians beliefs about the universe and regulated their rules of conduct and moral principles. The vizier, who controlled the law courts, had a figure of Maat as his badge of office and held the title 'Priest of Maat'. She was always present at the judgement of the dead when the heart of the deceased was weighed against her feather (see page 46)

HATHOR

She was a popular bovine goddess who was worshipped in three forms: as a cow, as a woman with the ears of a cow, and as a woman wearing a headdress of wig, horns and a sun disc. Her name means 'house of Horus' which was written in the form of a falcon within a hieroglyph

Figure 21 Hathor

33

representing a building (see Figure 21 top right-hand corner), and she was regarded as the divine mother of Horus (as was Isis). She was a goddess of the sky, and the pleasurable aspects of life such as love, beauty, joy, motherhood and music as well as foreign lands and turquoise mining. Her connection with music was represented by the sistrum, an instrument shaken by the priestess during religious ceremonies. One of her titles was 'Lady of the West'; it was believed that each evening she received the setting sun, which she protected until sunrise the following morning, in a similar way to Nut, goddess of the sky. The dying and deceased wanted her presence so that they would be similarly protected in the next life.

SEKHMET

Her name means 'she who is powerful'; she was the warrior lioness-goddess, often depicted as a woman with the head of a lioness and wearing a blood-red coloured dress. Lions were the fiercest hunter known to the Ancient Egyptians and during times of war, she protected the pharaoh in battle, launched fiery arrows at his enemies and sent them plagues, famine and illness.

Figure 22 Sekhmet

She was also regarded as a solar deity, being the daughter of the sun god Ra who personified aggression and revenge in her role as the fiery 'eye of Ra'. One of the legends regarding her ferocity was that her father Ra wanted to punish mankind for ignoring the gods, so he sent Sekhmet down to earth to wreak vengeance on them until they repented. Once on the earth, the vengeful goddess started to slaughter everyone, killing men, women, and children. Her blood thirst had no limits, and she almost exterminated the whole of humankind in one day. To stop her killing the rest of humanity the following day, while she slept the gods tricked her by mixing seven thousand jars of beer with red colouring and pouring it over the land. When she saw it she thought it was blood and gorged herself on it until she was drunk and passed out. Her mood had changed when she awoke, the killing was over!

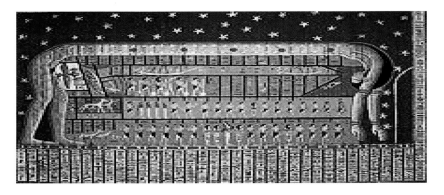

Figure 23 Nut tomb ceiling

NUT

Nut was the sky-goddess, mother of Osiris and Seth. She was usually shown in human form, her body arching over the earth, her limbs denoting each cardinal point. As a funerary deity, every evening she swallowed the setting sun that travelled the length of her body during the night, to be reborn from her womb the next morning. This nightly journey of the sun is commonly depicted on the ceilings of temples and royal tombs in the Valley of the Kings, and on the underside of the lid of coffins and sarcophagi; the deceased was meant to be inside the body of Nut, awaiting re-birth in the next life.

DEMONS

As well as a plethora of gods and goddesses, demons also affected the living. They lived at the edge of the created world as the forces of chaos, and some were called upon by Sekhmet to send terror and evil down on humanity. Terrifying demons occupied the Underworld through which the deceased had to travel; they cannot be regarded as evil as they were under the command of the gods, but they were very dangerous. One had a head that faced backwards, some had two heads and many carried weapons such as knives. They had grotesque and alarming names such as *'Blood-drinker who comes from the slaughterhouse'* and *'one who eats the*

Figure 24 Ammut

excrement of his hindquarters'. The best known of these Underworld beings was the female demon Ammut, the *'devourer of the dead'* depicted with the head of a crocodile, the foreparts of a lion and the rear of a hippopotamus. She ate the hearts of the 'bad' people who failed the 'Weighing of the Heart' test on judgement day.

The deities of Ancient Egypt, good and bad, were an integral part of their society and worship of them was part of the everyday life of commoners and royalty alike. Each city had a special, most revered god while acknowledging the existence of the others, but more importantly, their religion gave them a common purpose and they all subscribed to the same set of morals and ethics.

5   JOURNEY TO ETERNITY

Travel Instructions, Preparation and Packing

for the Great Journey!

The Ancient Egyptians believed in life after death and did everything they could to ensure that they had a happy and joyful Afterlife for all eternity. They prepared the body, followed specific 'travel' instructions, had rituals and ceremonies and finally, all their worldly goods were packed up for despatch with them.

INSTRUCTIONS

Much of what they did and said to facilitate the Journey was prescribed in the *Book of the Dead*, a funerary text from the Second Intermediate Period, but based on the earlier texts known as the *Pyramid Texts* and *Coffin Texts*. It is a collection of 189 spells and instructions, which they believed would guide and protect them through the Underworld

Figure 25 Book of the Dead, Papyrus of Ani

until they reached the Afterlife, which was a place of happiness where they would have a perfect eternal life. Several spells from *The Book of the Dead* were chosen by the deceased and placed with them inside the coffin, within the mummy bandages or rolled up and placed within a statuette of Sokar-Osiris. The spells were usually written on papyri in hieroglyphic, hieratic or demotic script.

PREPARATION

The Egyptians believed they needed their body intact in order to enjoy the Afterlife, so took great care in ensuring it was preserved for all time, or mummified. The term is misleading as it is taken from the Arabic word for bitumen or pitch, *'mummiya'*, which early Egyptologists believed covered the bodies of the deceased. A more accurate term is embalming which means to preserve (a corpse) with aromatic resins.

WHO WAS MUMMIFIED?
We believe that the practice of mummification began in the early 4th Dynasty (*c.*2615 BC) but recent evidence suggests that the evolution of embalming could have began as early as 4500 BC. Chemical analysis on linen body wrappings from that period indicates that they were soaked in preserving substances, similar to those used during the New Kingdom. Embalming was originally a privilege of royalty but as time passed, it was a process for everyone who could afford it. This included the elite of society such as court and government officials, scribes, high priests and men (and their families) who were at the top of their profession. An example is the beautiful tomb and well-preserved remains of Kha and his wife Merit at Deir el-Medina; he was a man of modest background who

rose in rank to become the overseer of construction of the royal tombs in the Valley of the Kings.

The whole process of mummification took up to seventy days, depending on the level of service paid for.

WHERE?
Soon after death, the body was taken to the Place of Purification, a simple structure of poles supporting a roof made from leaves or linen. It would have been sited near water and probably on the West bank of the Nile, which was associated with the setting sun and therefore death. It would have been on the outskirts of populated areas since the general population would not want to see or smell the process, a reminder of their own imminent death.

After the body had been purified with a solution of natron and water, it was taken to the embalming enclosure known as the 'House of Beauty' for the mummification procedures.

WHO DID IT?
A team of embalmers headed by the 'Controller of the Mysteries', a priest representing the jackal headed god Anubis, were responsible for the whole process. Anubis was the god of embalming and it was believed that he looked after the deceased during its Journey to Eternity. The priest wore an Anubis headdress, as shown in Fig. 26. Just as important was the Lector

Figure 26 Controller of the Mysteries

39

Priest who read out the prayers and magical incantations at every stage of the proceedings. These two main officiants supervised a group of technicians who mixed lotions, washed organs, heated resin and completed every other menial task the process entailed.

WHAT WAS DONE?

The Ancient Egyptians were aware that the putrefying process started in the internal organs so the first step was to remove all of them except the heart, which they believed was the centre of all thought and feeling.

REMOVAL OF THE BRAIN

The deceased was laid out on a wooden board, tilted at one end to allow the bodily fluids to flow out of the body, and the soft brain tissue was extracted. First, a sharp instrument was pushed up the left nostril to break through the ethmoid bone into the cranium. A hooked rod was poked into the cavity and swished around inside the skull until it liquefied the brain and it drained out through the nostrils. Any remaining brain matter was scooped out with a long-handled spoon. Occasionally, entry to the skull was through an eye socket or the back of the head. The skull was then packed with sawdust or resin soaked linen.

REMOVAL OF THE VISCERA

An incision was made in the left lower abdomen and the embalmer drew out the stomach, lungs, liver and intestines, but left the heart. Kidneys were sometimes removed but more often, left in place. Their significance is unknown but as there was not an Ancient Egyptian word for them, it is possible the embalmers did not know they existed!

Figure 27 Four sons of Horus canopic jars

The organs were then washed with water and natron, dried, anointed with sweet smelling oils and wrapped in linen bandages. They were placed in four separate vessels called canopic jars, representing four minor gods, the Sons of Horus; Imsety had the liver, Hapy the lungs, Duamutef the stomach and Qebehsenuef looked after the intestines. All were placed in the tomb near the body, often in a special box.

DRYING AND PACKING

After rinsing the inside of the body cavity with palm wine and spices it was packed with a temporary stuffing of rags, straw or wood-shavings, in fact, anything that was absorbent to help speed up the dehydration process. The body was then heaped with natron and left for forty days.

At the end of the dehydration period, the embalmer had to bring all his skills to bear to restore the deceased to an appearance as lifelike as possible. The temporary stuffing was removed, the body washed again and then re-packed with bags of natron and wads of linen soaked in sweet smelling resin, to help the body retain its shape. The whole body was then massaged several times with a moisturising lotion made of juniper oil, beeswax, spices, milk and wine, to bring the dry shrivelled skin back to its original soft and supple state. The incision in the abdomen was stitched and then covered with a *wedjat*-eye, a powerful symbol that averted evil and helped to magically heal the wound, before the body was then coated with molten resin which toughened it and made it waterproof.

Finally, before the body was wrapped in linen bandages, the embalmers carried out a few cosmetic procedures. Linen pads were placed under the skin of the face to improve its shrunken appearance, eyes were painted onto pads covering the eye sockets, make-up was applied to the cheeks and lips before finally a wig of human hair was placed on the head. The bodies of the wealthiest were also adorned with their favourite pieces of jewellery. Now the body could be wrapped in as many as twenty layers of bandages, which could take up to fifteen days. Every ritual was accompanied by magical words that had been prescribed in the *Book of the Dead*, and each layer was painted with molten resin to make the wrappings stick together.

At every stage of the wrapping, amulets were placed at specified positions as laid down in the funerary texts. Chapter 30B of the *Book of the Dead* stated that a scarab made from nephrite was placed over the heart (with a spell written on the back), and Chapter 155 was concerned with giving the backbone sufficient strength to raise up the body once more. By placing a *djed*–pillar at the throat of the deceased, (this represented the backbone of the god Osiris), the resurrected body would be able to rise again. Several hundred amulets have been found on a single body.

Figure 28 Djed-pillar

BURIAL

The body was now mummified and ready for burial, but before it was placed in a coffin, a mummy mask was placed over its head and shoulders. Usually made from cartonnage (linen stiffened with plaster), the wealthier would have some features decorated with gilding, and royalty such as Tutankhamun had masks made from solid gold. The purpose of the mask was to protect the head which was needed in the Afterlife, and to help the spirits of the deceased recognise the body when they returned to the burial chamber.

Coffins were rectangular boxes, generally made from wood and simply decorated with two *wedjat*-eyes and bands of hieroglyphs giving the deceased's name and titles and prayers to the gods. However, from the Middle Kingdom, human-form or anthropoid coffins were used and became the most popular style for the rest of the pharaonic period, developing more colour and decoration as time went on. Often, the mummy was placed inside a nest of coffins, each fitting neatly within the next before all were placed within a stone sarcophagus.

THE LAST RITES

Figure 29 Opening of the Mouth

This most important ritual was carried out in front of the tomb before placing the mummy inside. The Controller of the Mysteries, wearing the Anubis mask, held the mummy of the deceased upright while the priests said prayers, and held ritual implements towards the deceased to symbolically open the mouth and other senses. This ritual was meant to restore all

43

faculties and bodily functions to the spirit of the deceased so it could see, hear, smell, breathe and eat, and enjoy to the full all the Afterlife had to offer.

WORLDY GOODS
Once the coffin had been placed inside the tomb, the deceased's worldly goods were packed alongside it, together with food and drink. They believed that all the items used in normal daily life would be needed in the Afterlife, so they had to be taken with them. If the tomb was big enough they would take a full size bed and headrest, cupboards packed with clothes, shoes and jewellery, pots, knives, baskets and drinking vessels - anything and everything! The dead were expected to maintain the perfection of their heavenly paradise by ploughing the land, sowing and reaping so, from the Middle Kingdom, they took with them a figure called a *shabti* who would do the work for them. By the early New Kingdom, the *shabti*s were regarded as servants of the deceased who would do all the tasks necessary to maintain the land of paradise and provide the deceased with all his creature comforts by baking bread, weaving, brewing beer and all other menial tasks. Where previously one *shabti* was sufficient, the numbers gradually increased to 365 *shabtis*, one for each day of the year, and 36 overseer *shabtis* who carried whips to ensure there was no slacking!

Figure 30 Shabti

THE UNDERWORLD

After the body was placed in the tomb, friends and relatives made offerings of food and wine to the gods and the deceased, and then enjoyed a burial feast. The deceased was now on his journey through the Underworld, facing all the dangers and horrors detailed in the *Book of the Dead*. There were many books over the millennia which gave varying but similar descriptions of what to expect in the Underworld; the *Book of Gates, Book of Caverns, Coffin Texts,* and *Amduat* as well as the *Book of the Dead*.

The Underworld was not a hell to which souls were condemned but the place where a person's spirit went after death for judgement. It was the realm of Osiris, supernatural beings and other gods such as Anubis, Horus, Thoth, Hathor and Maat, who all appeared as the deceased made his way through the Underworld towards the final judgement.

There were realistic features like rivers, islands and fields along with fantastic lakes of fire, walls of iron and trees of turquoise. The deceased had to pass a series of gates guarded by dangerous spirits, some armed with weapons, and mounds and caverns inhabited by supernatural animals that threatened the spirits of the dead.

Once he had succeeded in overcoming all the perils and demons he met there, he had to have a final judgement, known as the Weighing of the Heart, before Osiris and forty-two judges representing different aspects of *maat*.

WEIGHING OF THE HEART

First, the deceased had to prove that he had been virtuous throughout his time on earth and was worthy of the honour of everlasting life. In an important element of the judgement ritual, the deceased called upon each judge by name and gave the relevant 'negative confession' such as: *'O Far Strider who came forth from Heliopolis, I have done no falsehood.'*

Thoth, the scribal god, waited with his pen and papyrus ready to record the verdict. Anubis the jackal god held the hand of the deceased to the left of the scales where the final act would take place, while the demon Ammut waited expectantly on the other side. An individual's heart was thought to be the centre of their intelligence and personality, so in accordance with funerary texts in *the Book of the Dead*, the heart was the focus of the final judgement. The heart of the deceased was weighed against *maat*, the feather of truth and justice. If the heart was as light as the feather, it proved that the deceased had been a good person; if it weighed heavier, they must have been bad. The good were given free passage into the Afterlife to live happily ever after; the hearts

Figure 31 Weighing of the Heart

of the bad were thrown to Ammut who hungrily devoured them, and that was a second and final death for the bad people!

THE AFTERLIFE

The Egyptians believed that three spirits were released at death; the *ka,* the *ba* and the *akh.*

The *ka,* which was represented by two upstretched arms, was the life force of the individual, the essential ingredient that differentiated a living person from a dead body. Created at the same time as the body, it was a

Figure 32 The *ka*

double of the living person but had no life of its own until the body died. It continued to live inside the tomb and needed sustenance in the form of food and drink, which was why relatives and friends would leave offerings outside the tomb. They believed that the *ka* would come out of the tomb through the False Door, and take the life-giving properties of the food offering (but not physically eat and drink).

The *ba* spirit embodied the individual traits and personality of the deceased that distinguished him from other people and made him unique. It was represented by a human headed bird and was far more versatile than the *ka.* The *ba* had the freedom to take on any form it wished to revisit the world of the living, but had to be reunited with the body every

Figure 33 The *ba* Spirit

night so that the physical body of the deceased could survive in the Afterlife.

The crested ibis represented a person's akh or immortality. This spirit was what we might refer to as the soul; it was the result of the successful union of the ba and the ka, severed all ties with the mortal remains of the deceased and inhabited the paradise of the Afterlife.

NOT JUST PEOPLE!

The Ancient Egyptians believed that their deities could appear on earth in the form of sacred animals; a cow for instance might really be the goddess Hathor, or the god Amun might disguise himself as a ram. Most animals were regarded as food, but any creature lucky enough to live within the temple precinct was regarded as a deity, and was therefore given a life of luxury. When it died it was embalmed and buried in royal fashion.

Figure 34 Mummified cats

Things got out of hand during the Late Period (c.670 BC). Every single creature that could be considered sacred, living in the temple or anywhere else, was embalmed and buried as if it was a god. Mummies have survived of fish, snakes, beetles, baboons and crocodiles, to name just a few. Thousands of animals were bred purely to supply the demand; pious people bought them to bury at the cult centres of their favourite deities. At Saqqara, underground rooms are stacked high with more than four million ibises, each in its own conical pottery jar, and tons of mummified cats were found at Speos Artemidos near Beni Hassan. The cats were shipped to Liverpool in 1890 to be turned into fertiliser.

The people of Ancient Egypt were mummified in order to achieve immortality. And they have, of a sort; we may not believe that they are up with the stars enjoying a heavenly Afterlife – but they are still here, over 3,000 years after they died, their names living on in ancient texts and their bodies still preserved in their mummified state.

6   GREAT PHARAOHS

Six 'Great' Pharaohs

Several pharaohs come to mind as being 'great', either for the length of their reign, their political and diplomatic achievements, the changes they imposed upon their subjects, or for the wonderful temples, palaces and tombs they left behind. This chapter describes the status and role of the pharaoh and a little about my choice of six 'great' pharaohs, in chronological order. The dates given refer to their reign rather than their life span.

The word 'pharaoh' derives from a respectful way of referring to the king of Egypt by describing him as the 'great house' (*per-ao*), meaning the palace where he lived. This name was used as the king's title from the late 18th Dynasty onwards but Greek usage eventually changed it into the word 'pharaoh'.

The Ancient Egyptians believed that the pharaoh was both mortal man and god. He was the falcon god Horus while he was alive on earth, then he became the god Osiris when his mortal body died and he lived for eternity with the other gods among the stars. This concept of kingship and the divinity of the pharaoh were central to Egyptian religion and society.

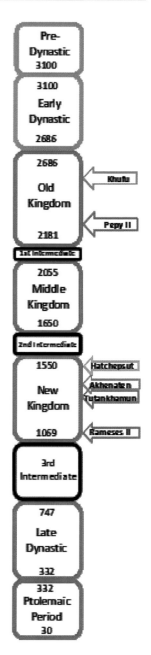

Pre-Dynastic
3100

3100
Early Dynastic
2686

2686
Old Kingdom
2181

Khufu

Pepy II

1st Intermediate

2055
Middle Kingdom
1650

2nd Intermediate

1550
New Kingdom
1069

Hatchepsut

Akhenaten
Tutankhamun

Rameses II

3rd Intermediate

747
Late Dynastic
332

332
Ptolemaic Period
30

From the Middle Kingdom (2055-1650 BC) onwards, it had been established that each pharaoh had a sequence of five names and titles; his birth name and four names which were given to him when

he became pharaoh. Three of his names emphasised his role as a god while the other two stressed the division of Egypt into two lands, both under his control. The two most important and regularly used names, which were written last in the sequence, were the name he was given at birth and one of the names he was given when he was crowned king (his

Figure 35 Birth and Throne names of Tutankhamun

throne name). From the 4th Dynasty onwards the birth name and the throne name were each enclosed in a cartouche, which represented a length of knotted rope and signified the concept of 'encircling protection', thereby protecting the name and person of the pharaoh. The two cartouches are usually displayed together; the two shown here contain the birth name of the pharaoh Tutankhamun which was Tut-ankh-amun Hekai-unu-shema, meaning "Living image of Amun, ruler of Upper Heliopolis" and his throne name Neb-kheperu-re meaning "Lord of the forms of Re" .

The other three king names, in order, were:

1. The **'Horus'** name. Horus was the falcon-god who was the embodiment of the reigning king's divinity and his protector. This name was written within a rectangular frame (*serekh*) representing the pharaoh's palace with the god Horus seated on top.
2. **'He of the Two Ladies'** name. The two ladies were the vulture goddess Nekhbet and the cobra goddess Wadyt, patron deities of Upper Egypt and Lower Egypt

respectively. The two goddesses appear on the pharaoh's crown as the double uraeus (protective symbol).

3. The **'Horus of Gold'** name. This name normally featured the image of a Horus falcon perched above or beside the hieroglyph for gold but its meaning is disputed. One belief is that gold was considered divine since it was eternal and therefore represented the pharaoh (Horus) living for all eternity. The other belief is that it represented Horus being triumphant over his enemies.

Ideally, the kingship passed from father to son, and although this was not always possible, the succeeding pharaoh was always keen to emphasise that he was the chosen heir to the throne, with a right to rule through his own divinity. The greatest of the pharaohs ruled Upper Egypt (the south) and Lower Egypt (the north), creating a unified and harmonious country which was the envy of many of its neighbours. In times of conflict, famine and pestilence, the country was not united, and struggled under separate rulers in the north and the south, and are referred to as the 'Intermediate Periods'.

As the representative of the gods on earth, the function of the pharaoh was to maintain and restore the original harmony that existed when the world was created – their 'world' being Egypt. Many of the drawings seen in temples, tombs and palaces were concerned with this overall responsibility, rather than depicting actual events throughout the king's lifetime. The idea of harmony, together with truth and justice was personified by the goddess Maat.

KHUFU (2589-2566 BC)

King Khufu, also known by his Greek name Cheops, was the second king of the 4th Dynasty in the Old Kingdom and builder of the iconic Great Pyramid at Giza, the last remaining of the Seven Wonders of the Ancient World. For that reason alone he is included in my list of 'great' pharaohs.

A pyramid is a funerary monument, built to house the mummified remains of the pharaoh in preparation for his journey to the Afterlife. Unfortunately, Khufu's remains were missing from his burial chamber within the pyramid when it was re-opened by the Arab caliph Abdullah al-Mamun around AD 820, it having been looted and emptied prior to the Middle Kingdom. Evidence suggests that construction began on Khufu's pyramid very soon after he took the throne and continued for almost the entire length of the king's reign. It was the tallest man-made structure in the world at 146 m and remained so for 3,800 years until the 160 m tall spire of Lincoln Cathedral was completed c.1311 AD. (see Chapter 9 Pyramids)

Khufu was reputed to have been a cruel and merciless ruler but that

cannot be substantiated by contemporary evidence, and was probably based on the scale of his pyramid and the number of men needed to build it. Khufu also built three queens' pyramids, several boat pits and a recently discovered small satellite pyramid. The size and numbers may indicate that Khufu was a great organiser and leader rather than a merciless tyrant.

Figure 36 King
Khufu

Despite having the biggest and most famous funerary complex in Egypt, the only known three dimensional representation of Khufu is an 8 cm ivory statue of him seated on a throne and wearing the red crown of Lower Egypt. It was excavated from the temple of Khentimentiu at Abydos and is currently held in the Museum of Egyptian Antiquities, Cairo.

PEPY II (2278-2184 BC)

Pepy II is included here in the 'greats' because of his exceedingly long reign. He ruled during the 6th Dynasty (the final dynasty of the Old Kingdom), and was the longest reigning pharaoh throughout all of Egypt's ancient history. He came to the throne when he was about ten years old and was still pharaoh 94 years later, possibly the longest reigning monarch the world has ever known!

Pepy II is noted for developing new trade links with southern Africa, maintaining diplomatic and commercial relations with Byblos in ancient Syria/Palestine and a policy of peaceful trading in Nubia.

However, increasing power and wealth were handed over to high government officials during his kingship. He further decentralised power away from the capital Memphis (and therefore the throne) by splitting the role of

Figure 37 Pepy II with his Mother

vizier into two, one for Upper Egypt and the other for Lower Egypt. It is probable that these decisions, together with his very long reign, contributed to the gradual demise of the Old Kingdom. They allowed the pharaoh's power to be weakened, the administration to stagnate and possibly produced a succession crisis; the heirs he appointed probably died before him, leaving various rivals in contention for the throne. The period which followed the Old Kingdom, the First Intermediate Period (2181-2055 BC), was a time of instability and relative political disunity, with a rapid succession of rulers, all of which undermined royal authority.

He was buried in his pyramid complex at Saqqara (see Chapter 9 The Pyramids) which was the last great royal building project of the era, probably because the ability to command material and labour on such a huge scale had passed beyond royal control.

HATSHEPSUT (1473-1458 BC)

Hatshepsut was the 6th ruler of the 18th Dynasty, a female who overturned tradition by declaring herself a pharaoh, and proved herself to be more than capable of the role – a true 'great'. In order to discover how she made this remarkable move we need to take a brief look at her family history.

She married her half-brother Thutmose II, when they were both about twelve years of age. He had been crowned pharaoh, and in accordance with tradition she married him and became his co-regent. Two years after their union, she gave birth to their daughter, Neferura. When her husband died a few years later in 1479 BC, the son of her husband's minor wife Aset, being the only male child, was declared heir to the throne and the future pharaoh Thutmosis III. He married his half-sister Neferura (Hatshepsut's daughter) to help reinforce his position. Since he was too young to rule, Hatshepsut was appointed regent.

Figure 38 Hatshepsut

So far, she had done exactly what had been expected of her. However, after seven years as a dutiful regent she adopted all the titles of a king, wore male clothes and a false beard (this represented the pharaoh's status as a living god) and declared herself the true pharaoh of all Egypt. She effectively blocked Thutmosis III from taking power; she wanted to be seen as the rightful heir, the chosen one of the gods.

To further emphasise her rightful position and her divine birth, she stated on her temple wall that the god Amun took the form of her human father, impregnated her mother and she was the result, the offspring of a god. She also had carved into the walls a proclamation from her father that she should be his sole heir. It is highly unlikely that her father had done this but it was a useful political tool.

She was not always shown as a man; she described herself as a beautiful woman and liked to show her beauty and femininity, keeping the male attire for official duties. Her closest advisor (and lover according to graffiti of the time) was Senenmut, chief steward and tutor of her daughter. Hatshepsut commissioned numerous building projects, with Senenmut as the architect and overseer, many of them at the Temple of Amun at Karnak. Still standing is one of two obelisks she had erected there in honour of her father, the god Amun. It is 28.5 m tall, beautifully carved, and was originally covered in electrum (a natural alloy of gold and silver). It would have glowed like a beacon in the moonlight and would have been dazzling in the sunshine, a fitting tribute to the sun god. Once again, Hatshepsut was emphasising that Amun was her father and

Figure 39 Mortuary Temple, Deir el-Bahri

therefore she was the rightful pharaoh.

Her most famous building, and one of the most visited ancient Egyptian sites, is her mortuary temple at Deir el Bahri. It is built into the limestone cliff-face that soars 300 m above the desert floor, and is an awesome sight when viewed from the long, straight road leading to its magnificent terraces. It looks quite modern, with its geometric formality, and is dramatically different from other New Kingdom temples. The temple itself is about 100 m wide and 30 m high with three terraces, shrines, courtyards supported by columns, and chapels to the gods.

As well as all the building activity during her reign, Hatshepsut expanded Egyptian territory and broadened its trading links, noting on the walls of her temple the trading expeditions to Punt, Byblos and Sinai. The expedition to the Land of Punt (possibly near present day Somalia) seems to have been particularly memorable; the fleet of five ships she sent in 1493 BC brought back such luxury items as incense, ebony, ivory and animal skins. It has been suggested that her reign was exceptionally peaceful but new evidence indicates that she continued to send out military expeditions when necessary. She disappeared from the records when she was about 40 years old when her husband Thutmosis III eventually took over the throne as sole ruler. It is not known if she had died at that time or been removed from power. She had a tomb built for herself in the Valley of the Kings, tomb KV20, but there is no evidence that she was actually buried there. She proved to be an equal among the male pharaohs, and a big improvement on most of them!

AKHENATEN (1352-1336 BC)

I consider Akhenaten 'great' for his infamy as the 'heretic' king who revolutionised the religion and art of Egypt during his kingship. He was the son of Amenhotep III and Queen Tiy and was originally known as Pharaoh Amenhotep IV when he succeeded to the throne.

Figure 40 Akhenaten

During the first year of his reign, he established a temple at Karnak dedicated to the sun disc Aten, in preference to the god Amun. Four years later he made the crucial decision to change his name from Amenhotep (meaning *Amun is content*) to Akhenaten (*glory of the sun disc*), and began the construction of a new capital city called Akhetaten (*horizon of the Aten)*, now known as Tell el-Amarna. This new city was intended to replace both Thebes and Memphis as the centre for administration and religious focus.

He vigorously promoted the worship of the Aten to the exclusion of all other deities, even eradicating their names from temple walls in an attempt to have the Aten recognised as a single supreme deity. This phase in Egyptian history is described as the Amarna period and covers the style of art that Akhenaten introduced as well as the change in religious worship. The Aten sun disc with rays reaching out holding the symbol of life, the *ankh*, is a typical symbol of the time and appears in most reliefs.

Traditional Egyptian art was most concerned with depicting the continuity of the universe, the gods,

Figure 41 The Aten

the king and his people. Therefore they were depicted, not as the artists saw them, but as idealised versions of the real world. Human figures were carved and painted with a formulaic precision, always showing the pharaoh and his queen as young, healthy, virile and beautiful. Akhenaten completely transformed the style. The statuary, paintings and reliefs of

Figure 42 Akhenaten, Nefertiti and children with the Aten

his period were characterised by an emphasis on the god Aten and the royal family. He, together with his wife Nefertiti and their young daughters were shown in unusually warm, intimate family scenes, which were unprecedented in Ancient Egyptian culture. They were depicted with unusual facial and bodily features, such as elongated skull, face, limbs and fingers together with protruding belly and heavy thighs, all of which give a distorted image of the average human form. However, there is some evidence that suggests certain physical features were due to inherited medical conditions and there is the possibility that the family looked as they were depicted.

There is evidence of the pharaoh's relationship with states in Asia from the Amarna Letters. These form diplomatic correspondence written between Akhenaten and the great powers of Western Asian states such as Babylonia and Assyria, and the vassal states of Syria and Palestine. They are written in Akkadian, the international language of the day, on 382 clay tablets. It seems that Akhenaten was neglectful of the vassal states as their letters become increasingly desperate for his assistance as their cities fell under siege.

His reign is regarded as 'unsuccessful' since his son Tutankhamun subsequently reversed all the changes he had brought about.

TUTANKHAMUN (1336-1327 BC)

I have included Tutankhamun as a 'great' pharaoh, not for what he achieved (not a lot!) but for the wonderful legacy he left behind in the form of exquisite treasures found in his tomb, one of which is detailed in Treasures of Ancient Egypt (Chapter 11).

Figure 43 Tutankhamun

Known as the 'boy king', Tutankhamun came to the throne at 8 years of age following the death of his father Akhenaten and died himself nine years later. At the behest of his highest court officials who guided and taught the young king in his pharaonic duties, he quickly restored all the old deities to their previous top position at the heart of religion and society. His father's new religion had not won favour with the general populace and especially not with the priests who had lost their livelihood, so this reversal to the old ways made the young king very popular.

His father was Akhenaten and for years it was assumed that his mother was Kiya, one of Akhenaten's secondary wives. However, recent scientific evidence from the mummified remains of a young unnamed female found in tomb KV35, known as The Younger Lady, indicate that this woman was his mother. Genetic fingerprinting and tests on mitochondrial DNA prove that Tutankhamun's mother was also his aunt, his father Akhenaten's sister. Incest was a common occurrence within royal circles since they believed it kept their bloodline pure; the opposite is true and probably led to many inherited genetic problems.

So what did Tutankhamun look like? This is a reconstruction of his head by the forensic anthropologist Jean-Noël Vignal, and the forensic sculptor, Elisabeth Daynès taken from Tutankhamun's mummified remains.

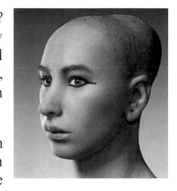

Figure 44 Reconstruction of Tutankhamun's Skull

He was 180 cm in height, quite tall for an Egyptian of this period, and of slim build. He had a slight curvature of the spine, and a clubfoot which meant he walked with great difficulty using a stick (130 were found in his tomb). He was married to Ankhensenamun, his half-sister whose mother was Nefertiti, the first and Great Wife of Akhenaten. They had two daughters who were both stillborn; their mummified remains were found in his tomb.

Scientific research into the possible causes of his death has resulted in several theories; he was murdered by a blow to the head, he was crushed by a chariot or he died from a combination of several genetic conditions and diseases. However, recent evidence proves that his left femur was broken just above the knee, a serious trauma which probably killed him. It is the only bone fracture that happened prior to his death with all other breaks, for example to his head (the murder theory), and to his pelvis and chest (the chariot accident theory), all now believed to be post mortem.

He was first known as Tutankhaten (*living image of the Aten*) but later changed his name to Tutankhamun in order to associate himself more closely with his re-instatement of Amun as the principal god. He moved the royal court from Akhetaten back to Memphis and erected a 'restoration stela' detailing the reforms he had authorised to undo the unpopular excesses of his father's reign.

He was practically unknown to Egyptologists before Howard Carter discovered his tomb in the Valley of the Kings (KV62) in 1922. The tomb had been partially robbed in ancient times but most of the funerary equipment was in excellent condition, the best preserved of any treasure found in a royal tomb. When his benefactor Lord Carnarvon asked "Can you see anything?" as the tomb was opened, Carter replied with the famous words: "Yes, wonderful things!"

RAMESES II (1279 -1213 BC)

Also known as Rameses the Great, he was the third ruler of the 19th

Dynasty in the New Kingdom and enjoyed a long reign of 66 years. He is often regarded as the greatest, most celebrated, and most powerful pharaoh of Ancient Egypt. His successors and later Egyptians called him the 'Great Ancestor'.

Before he came to the throne, he married Nefertari, who then reigned with him for 26 years as his Great Royal Wife. She seems to have been the best loved of all queens, working with her husband as a true colleague and confidante. In the early years of their relationship, she was depicted with him in statues as shown here at the Luxor Temple. This was typical of

Figure 45 Rameses II with Nefertari, Karnak

pharaonic statuary with Rameses a gigantic figure, representing his power and authority, while Nefertari was shown as a tiny form in front of him. In later years however, he dedicated the Hathor Temple at Abu Simbel to her where her statues are as tall as those of her husband and the goddess Hathor. As her final resting place, he had built for her the most spectacular and astonishingly beautiful tomb in the Valley of the Queens (QV66).

Figure 47 Hathor Temple, Abu Simbel

Rameses II is known for his extensive building programs and for the many colossal statues of him found all over Egypt. The building work which was completed during his reign was unprecedented; vast amounts of construction work were carried out during his kingship consisting of temples, monuments and statuary that included several rock-cut temples in Nubia at Abu Simbel and Gerf Hussein. In Egypt itself, he built numerous temples at Memphis, the court and pylon at Luxor temple, a temple at Abydos, and completed the decoration of the great hypostyle hall at Karnak.

Figure 46 The Battle of Kadesh, Rameses II Temple, Abu Simbel

He led several military expeditions into the Levant, reasserting Egyptian control over Canaan and led expeditions to the south, into Nubia, commemorated in inscriptions at Beit el-Wali and Gerf Hussein. The major event of his reign however, which was celebrated repeatedly on his major temples, was the Egyptian army's confrontation with the Hittites (people from Anatolia), known as the Battle of Kadesh. It was not the great victory Rameses would have hoped for (both sides claimed to have won) but it ensured that the Hittite empire was kept at bay and protected Egyptian interests in the Levant. He subsequently signed a treaty with the Hittite king Muwatallis and further consolidated good relations with the Hittite empire through his marriages to two Hittite princesses.

The Ramesseum, located on the west bank of the Nile opposite modern day Luxor, was the mortuary temple of Rameses II. The reliefs and architecture constitute an important source of information and evidence regarding the beliefs and rituals of the royal funerary cult.

His tomb is in the Valley of the Kings (KV7) and is an appropriate size for a king of his power. One of the largest tombs in the Valley, it covers 686 sq.m. Unfortunately, over the centuries the tomb has suffered a series of torrential floods that have washed tons of debris into the chambers, seriously damaging the walls and pillars. Despite the best efforts of at least ten archaeologists over the past 250 years, the tomb has not yet been cleared and it seems very unlikely that it will be cleared and opened to the public in the near future.

7 INFLUENTIAL QUEENS

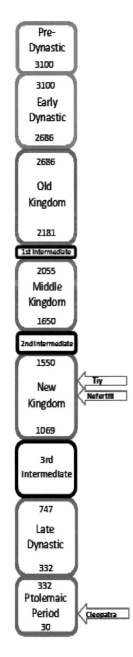

Three Powerful Queens

In ancient times, as now, many wives were the unacknowledged 'power behind the throne' who supported their husband in quiet, unobtrusive ways, giving guidance and advice to enable their husband achieve success. But in this chapter I want to focus on a few Ancient Egyptian queens who were exceptional and acknowledged as having great influence, not only on the man in their life but on the whole nation. The women who I believe qualify are Hatshepsut who is discussed in Chapter 4 Great Pharaohs, Tiy, Nefertiti and Cleopatra VII. With the exception of Cleopatra who was the last of the Ptolemaic queens in Egypt before the Romans took over, they lived during the New Kingdom, a very affluent time that lasted 500 years from about *c.*1500 BC.

The conventions of Egyptian art and literature focus mainly on the exploits of the king, therefore very little information regarding even the most famous of queens has survived. No matter how powerful or influential they were, they remain insubstantial figures, overshadowed by the dominant iconography of the pharaoh. Here I will bring together the knowledge we have on the three individuals, but I will start by looking at the normal or usual role of a queen, so that a comparison can be made with my three 'special' queens.

Who could be called queen? The lady chosen to be the pharaoh's first wife, either by him or advisors within the court, was given the title Great Royal Wife, and was Queen of Egypt. The pharaoh would have several minor wives and a harem of young women (including foreign princesses), but none of them seem to have carried the title of queen.

The only other woman to be given the title was the king's mother, who was greatly respected due to her maternal position. Because the pharaoh was believed to be the son of a god, it was also believed that the sun god Amun-Re (in the guise of her husband) had impregnated his mother. When her son, rather than any other son of the pharaoh, was crowned king, she was awarded the title of queen.

Together with the pharaoh, the queen was regarded as divine, which was demonstrated by the titles she held and the symbols of queenship and divinity she wore. One of the titles some queens took was 'God's Wife', which emphasised her husband's divinity and consequently her own – if he was a god then she must be a goddess!

Officially, it was the queen's role in society to support the pharaoh in all his kingly decisions, to bear his children (preferably a son and heir) and take part in the rituals of the temple as the wife and goddess of the king (god). The queen also had to be seen to epitomise femininity and all the good qualities of a wife and mother.

The three women detailed here fulfilled the official role admirably but they all had several other things in common: they were intelligent, focussed, ambitious, determined, powerful and, in one case in particular, quite ruthless. These traits, combined with beauty, charm and loyalty created a very heady and irresistible mix that they used to advantage on everyone within their circle of influence.

QUEEN TIY (1410-1340 BC)

Not to be confused with Tiy, a minor wife of Rameses III who conspired with officials of the harem to have him killed and her son Pentwere crowned in his place. The plot was discovered and she was sentenced to death.

Tiy was a commoner by birth; her father Yuya was a wealthy landowner from Upper Egypt where he served as a high priest and chariot officer and her mother Tuyu may have been a priestess with close links to the royal family. Some academics have suggested that Tiy was of Nubian origin but the more interesting aspect of her life is not where she came from but what she became.

Queen Tiy was the Great Wife of the 18th Dynasty ruler, Amenhotep III (1390-1352 BC) who ruled for 38 years with Tiy constantly by his side, their reign marked by the high standard of its artistic and architectural achievements and the opulence of the royal court. Their time in power was a period of unprecedented prosperity when Egypt reached the peak of its international power.

Figure 48 Queen Tiy

This small statuette of her (25 cm) was probably produced in her later years since the queen is shown at an advanced age with all the marks of her personality etched into her face: intelligence, determination and assertiveness.

Tiy seems to have exerted considerable influence on her husband, becoming his trusted adviser and confidante. She worked with the court officials and scribes overseeing the administrative aspects of the empire and its international affairs, while he concentrated on numerous building projects, erecting great monuments, temples and palaces. Tiy was regularly depicted in sculptures alongside her husband and he had a large temple built for her at Sedinga in Nubia. Amenhotep III was not interested in military campaigns, preferring to maintain the order established by his predecessors, with Tiy admirably filling the roles of negotiator and diplomat. Being wise, intelligent and strong, she gained the respect of foreign leaders and dignitaries who were happy to deal directly with her. For a woman to have such an important political role was rare, and almost unbelievable in the foreign countries she dealt with. Queen Tiy wielded as much power as her husband the pharaoh, far more than any other queen before her, and was the first Egyptian queen to have her name recorded on official acts.

She survived Amenhotep by twelve years and continued to play an active role in foreign relations. After her husband's death the correspondence from Tushratta, ruler of Mitanni (western Asia) was addressed directly to her, and Amarna letter EA26, which is addressed to her personally, dates to the reign of her son Akhenaten, who succeeded Amenhotep III. She continued to be mentioned in letters and inscriptions as 'queen and beloved of the king'.

A cache of royal mummies was found in the tomb of Amenhotep II (KV35) when Victor Loret opened it in 1898. Among others, it contained the remains of The Younger Lady (now identified as the mother of Tutankhamun) and another unnamed female mummy, called The Elder Lady by Egyptologists. In 2010, DNA analysis was able to formally identify the Elder Lady to be Queen Tiy. Strands of her brown wavy hair found inside a keepsake miniature coffin inside Tutankhamun's tomb matched the DNA of the Elder Lady, providing additional evidence of her identity and confirming her as Tutankhamun's grandmother.

Queen Tiy proved herself to be a woman of great presence and authority who exercised her power and influence in equal measure with the 'great' kings of Ancient Egypt.

QUEEN NEFERTITI (1380-1340 BC)

She was the Great Wife of Tutankhamun's father Akhenaten (Amenhotep IV) and the mother of his six daughters. Her name means 'the beautiful one has come'. This limestone bust of her was found in the workshop of the sculptor Thutmose in the city of Tell el-Amarna, the capital founded by her husband, and confirms she was as beautiful as her name suggests. Even in the ancient world, she was recognised as being the most beautiful of Egyptian queens.

Figure 49 Queen Nefertiti

Her husband is known as the 'heretic pharaoh', who replaced all the known and loved gods that had dominated Egypt for millennia, with one god, the sun disc Aten. In the old traditional religion only the pharaoh had a relationship with the gods, but under the new religion, the relationship was expanded to include the queen. It has been suggested that it was Nefertiti who persuaded her husband to take the course of action he did with the religion of the country, and therefore should possibly be known as the 'heretic queen'. The radical change in Egyptian theology reduced the power of the priesthood, previously second only to the king in matters of religion, and greatly increased her own power, authority and influence over matters of state. Her mother-in-law was Queen Tiy who visited the royal couple at Tell el-Amarna; it is possible that Nefertiti was influenced by her and built upon the achievements of that remarkable woman.

In artwork, her status is evident and indicates that she probably had as much, if not more influence than her husband. In the sixth year of his reign, he built a temple to the Aten that is dominated by reliefs and statues of Nefertiti. She is often shown officiating at religious ceremonies, with equal status with the king and she is depicted nearly twice as often in reliefs as her husband. She is even shown in the conventional pose of a pharaoh smiting the enemy. No other queen was ever shown so frequently on monuments, in temples and in statuary as Queen Nefertiti.

Despite all her power and influence, she seems to have receded into obscurity, or died, in the twelfth year of Akhenaten's reign, her role filled by her daughter Meritaten and another queen, Kiya. She was probably buried in the royal tomb to the east of Tell el-Amarna with her husband but no traces of royal mummies have survived at this site.

QUEEN CLEOPATRA VII (51-30 BC)

Figure 50 Elizabeth Taylor as Cleopatra

Cleopatra VII Philopater was the illustrious daughter of Pharaoh Ptolemy XII born in 69 BC; she was the last queen of Egypt. Shakespeare described her as a stunning woman whose infinite beauty "beggar'd all description" and Chaucer, writing in the 14th century, described her as "fair as is the rose in May." Obviously, they had never met her and they wrote what they imagined she looked like. However, Roman writers were familiar with her, and describe her as intelligent and charismatic with a seductive voice but, tellingly, they do not mention her beauty. The image of Cleopatra as a beautiful seductress is a more recent image and this coin, minted during her reign, is probably a more realistic portrait of her. She may not have been a great beauty but the fact that Cleopatra was charismatic, intelligent and able to speak eight languages, including the native language of Egypt, were more enduring qualities to have.

Her life story however, is one of family feuds, murder, great loves and finally, a tragic end.

In accordance with tradition, she married her half-brother Ptolemy XIII when he was ten years old and she was a young woman of nineteen, becoming co-regent and securing the

Figure 51 Coin with Cleopatra's head

throne for her family of Greek pharaonic rulers. However, with the advice and help of his supporters, Ptolemy quickly ousted her from power and she fled to Syria with her half sister Arsinoë.

Having previously formed a friendship with Cleopatra's father, the Roman general Pompey took refuge in Egypt after his defeat by Caesar at the Battle of Pharsalus. He expected a warm welcome from his old friend's children, his ward Cleopatra and her brother Ptolemy XIII and half sister Arsinoë. But Ptolemy, hoping to curry favour with Caesar, had Pompey arrested and killed. When the Roman general Caesar arrived in Egypt to visit her brother, he was presented with the head of Pompey on a platter. Caesar was angry at the insult afforded to Pompey, a great military and political leader of Rome, and the husband of his daughter Julia, and gave the remains of Pompey a correct Roman burial. Cleopatra heard news of Caesar's displeasure with Ptolemy and immediately returned, sensing she could use it to her advantage, and was smuggled into his chambers by her supporters, allegedly wrapped in a carpet. Having seduced him, she persuaded Caesar to reinstate her on the throne of Egypt. Nine months later she bore him a son, Ptolemy Caesar, known as Caesarion (little Caesar). Her husband Ptolemy XIII meanwhile had been killed in battle with Caesar's army and for political reasons she married her younger brother, Ptolemy XIV who was aged thirteen and again, she was co-regent and ruling Egypt.

Soon afterward, Caesar returned to Rome and Cleopatra followed him with their baby son where they all lived together as a family. After two years the political tide turned against Caesar and he was murdered, stabbed to death on the Ides of March 44 BC. Cleopatra immediately returned to Egypt with Caesarion and weeks later her brother and husband Ptolemy XIV died aged sixteen; it was strongly believed that Cleopatra had poisoned him. Within a very short time, she had proclaimed her son Caesarion the rightful pharaoh, with herself as co-regent, of course!

Figure 52 Mark Antony

Next on the political stage was the man who was probably the true love of her life, the Roman general Mark Antony, since by all accounts he and Cleopatra seem to have been very much in love and had a warm, affectionate and fun relationship. They met in 41 BC when Cleopatra was twenty-eight and Mark Antony was forty-two, and they went on to have a family; twins, a boy and a girl, Alexander and Cleopatra. They had a marriage ceremony, although Mark Antony was already married to a Roman woman, and four years later she gave birth to another son Ptolemy Philadelphus.

In 34 BC in the 'Donations of Alexandria', Mark Antony divided various parts of the eastern Roman Empire between Cleopatra and their children, telling Rome that he was simply installing client rulers. After a propaganda campaign led by his Roman brother-in-law, Octavian, he was summoned back to Rome but refused to return which resulted in the Roman authorities declaring war on him and Cleopatra.

He was defeated at the naval battle of Actium and, rather than be captured, took his own life. Cleopatra was distraught at losing him and, rather than face the humiliation of a Roman triumph in Egypt killed herself by holding an asp to her breast and dying from its poison.

But what of her half sister Arsinoë and her four children? Arsinoë was granted refuge in the Temple or Artemis at Ephesus by Caesar where she lived for several years. Her safety was short-lived however as she was murdered on the steps of the temple on the orders of Mark Antony (at Cleopatra's instigation). She is believed to have been buried in a tomb there but the evidence is inconclusive. Caesarion, aged seventeen when his mother died, was captured and executed by the Romans. The younger three were taken back to Rome where they were paraded through the streets of Rome in chains before being placed in the care of Mark Antony's Roman widow. The twins were ten years old and Ptolemy Philadelphus was six.

The young Cleopatra was later given in marriage to the King of Mauretania and lived until she was thirty-four. Alexander died aged fifteen, and young Ptolemy Philadelphus only lived a year in Rome before he died.

Cleopatra's life was filled with intrigue, plotting and murder, which is surprising considering her wealth of talents; she could have been the most successful queen in all of Ancient Egypt's long history if she had been more politically astute in her handling of Rome (and its generals). Instead, she is known as the last queen, her Egyptian empire lost to Rome through the choices she made, her great power and influence wasted.

8   MAGIC AND MEDICINE

Which One to Choose?

If Egypt is a land of mystery and magic today, it was even more so in ancient times. This chapter will reveal some of their mystical practices, explain why they believed their magic worked, tell you which medical procedures were successful, and give you recipes for magical potions and medical prescriptions. It is probably best not to try them at home!

Magic and medicine were intertwined and it is often difficult to differentiate between them since certain elements were the same. They were both part of the same belief system which was based on the Creation Gods who had made everything at the beginning of time. The gods made the sun, the moon, the stars and heavens, in fact, all natural things. Every aspect of life, every word, ritual, plant, animal and human being was connected to the power and authority of the deities. Therefore, whenever a person performed magic or practiced medicine, it was only possible through the power of the gods. Magic and medicine both had rituals, actions to be done and words to be chanted, and they both had special ingredients to make into potions. But before an afflicted person chose magic or medicine to cure their problems, they had to decide why they were suffering. Was it a run of bad luck, a physical injury or ailment, or an unknown malaise?

MAGIC

People would seek out the local magician for a spell or potion if they thought they were suffering a phase of 'bad luck', brought on because they had offended the gods in some way. They would repent (even when they did not know what they had done wrong), and they would plead with, cajole, flatter, threaten and lie to the gods, often all in the same spell. This did not always appease the gods but sometimes, seemingly, put a stop to their run of bad luck. Ill-fortune could also have been caused by the magical power of a foreign sorcerer, a demon or spirit of the dead, doing it simply because they enjoyed being evil – again, magic was used to counter the spell.

The Ancient Egyptian word for magic was *heka,* which means 'using the *ka'* or using 'divine force' and Figure 53 is the hieroglyph. This was one of the forces used by the gods to make the world, creating order out of chaos. In a text known as the *"Instruction for Merikara"* from *c.*2000 BC, *heka* was described as a

gift from the creator gods to humanity 'to ward off the blows of fate'. Strangely, the similar sounding verb 'hex' used in English and of Germanic origin, means to bewitch or put a spell on someone.

Figure 53
heka sign

The Egyptian god of magic was consequently named Heka and he was depicted in human form, holding a serpent in each hand. According to one of their myths, the god Heka fought and conquered two serpents and thereafter two intertwined serpents became symbolic of his power. This symbol, central to the hieroglyph for *heka,* is still associated today with 'good magic' i.e. medicine, and is still used today by some medical associations as their emblem. No major temples were built to honour Heka but shrines and priests were dedicated to him in Lower Egypt.

As well as being the creative force of gods, *heka* was the destructive force of demons. All supernatural beings possessed *heka* as did the pharaoh who would transfer some of his power to the temple priests who practised the art of magic. Any part of the king, e.g. hair and nail clippings, also had *heka,* and had to be kept in a safe place. If they got into the wrong hands, they could be used in magic against him (similar to voodoo). Any person considered different in some way, such as a dwarf, was considered to have *heka*, as were the spirits of the dead. A few other people possessed the power of *heka*: the scorpion charmer, who dealt with scorpion and snakebites and the 'wise woman' of the village, usually an elderly woman who would create spells and potions and give wise words of advice. In medieval England she would probably have been branded a witch.

The appeal of magic was that it identified the cause of problems and gave people hope in even the most desperate situation. It worked because they believed in its power and 'protective magic' gave people the comfort of knowing they had taken every possible precaution to prevent the mishaps and tragedies that came their way.

PROTECTIVE GODS
Some gods were regarded as being more sympathetic to the human condition and were invoked more regularly than others. A favourite deity was the goddess Isis who seems to have been the divinity most sympathetic to human suffering, and the goddess most willing to help the humblest members of society; one of her titles was 'The Saviour'.

Figure 54 Taweret

Figure 55 Bes

Hathor, often depicted as a cow or shown as a beautiful female with cow's ears, was the ultimate goddess. She represented lovemaking, fertility and motherhood and was the aspirational model for all Egyptian women who sought her protection in all female matters. Specific gods were called upon to protect the most vulnerable members of society, pregnant women and young children. The goddess Taweret, a curious mix of hippopotamus, lion and crocodile with flat, pendulous human breasts, was a favourite protector of pregnant women.

Small statues of Bes, a dwarf god with a lion's mane, were placed around the home and his image was painted on beds, cots and the walls of the house. He was meant to scare off any demons that threatened their safety.

MAGICIANS' EQUIPMENT

Like magicians today, the ancient practitioners of the art displayed an element of showmanship when they cast their magical spells.

They often carried a 'serpent rod' as an indication of their status and used an apotropaic (averting evil) wand to mark out their 'magic' circle in the sand. Within the circle the area had to be purified and fumigated with incense (to rid the ground of insects) and fresh sand was put down, all to create a sacred zone. Magical emblems would be placed all around the circle, which protected the inner circle and all that happened there.

The magician made use of many different amulets representing the gods he wished to call upon with his spells. Examples include the *wedjat*-eye, representing the left eye of the god Horus, which was particularly powerful, and the cat representing the goddess Bastet which protected against snakes. He would call upon the gods and goddesses by name while wafting the smoke from burning incense. It was believed the gods liked the perfumed air and would enter the 'magic' zone. The magician sometimes wore a mask, representing a particular god, while he chanted his spell. They believed that he would 'become' the god while he wore it which would make the magic more powerful. Masks similar to this, representing the jackal god Anubis, were worn by the

Figure 56 Anubis mask

Controller of the Ceremonies during the rites and rituals of mummification. Anubis was the god of mummification and the deity who protected the deceased during the journey to the Afterlife.

MAGICAL SYMBOLISM

The magician would sing or chant the words of the spell (to distinguish it from normal speech) and draw words and pictures in the sand of the inner circle. They believed that once images had been drawn the essence of them could be brought to life. They also had a special hand gesture they used in times of crisis, such as the birth of a child or animal, or when cattle were being driven across crocodile infested waters. The magician would clench his hand, hold the thumb and forefinger together and point at the problem, while chanting a spell.

The Egyptians credited certain colours with luck; red (the colour of blood and life), black and green (the colours of the alluvial soil, growth and regeneration) and blue (a heavenly colour, good for invoking the gods). The colour red however, could also be regarded as unlucky. It is a very potent colour, symbolising two extremes: life and power, as well as anger and fire. It was the colour of the desert and its destructive god Seth (who reputedly had red hair). 'Making red' implied killing someone but a special spell could be protective: *"Oh, Isis, deliver me from the hands of all bad, evil, red things."*

There were lucky and unlucky days (known as 'the days of the demons'), so the magician consulted a calendar before carrying out a spell, only doing them on auspicious days. The numbers four and seven seem to have been regarded as particularly lucky since many of the spells had to be recited either four or seven times. The time of the day was just as important, with dawn and dusk being the most favourable times for magic to work.

OTHER FORMS OF MAGIC

The magicians practiced the art of divination, where they attempted to foretell future events or discover hidden knowledge to answer the questions their clients put to them. The ceremony usually involved a lighted candle in a dark room, a bowl of oil to gaze into (similar to a crystal ball) and a young boy who would be able to 'see' the future when prompted by the magician.

The Egyptians also believed in speaking to the deceased or 'dangerous dead'. I refer to them as 'dangerous' because the Egyptians believed that the dead, especially women, caused bad things to happen to the living - it wasn't just demons who brought them diseases and bad luck. Women had the reputation for being jealous of the living and very vindictive over wrongs and slights they felt people had done to them during their lifetime. So they wrote letters, on pots and bowls, to their friendly deceased relatives, asking them to intercede on their behalf with the 'dangerous dead'. One letter on a pot in the Petrie Museum is from a widow to her dead brother asking him to intervene on behalf of her daughter as the dead were acting 'evilly' towards her; she wanted him to find out who it was and to stop them.

Dreams were also regarded as having a 'magical' element, with magicians having the power to interpret their meaning after consulting a 'Dream Book'. In general, the dream books contained about one hundred dreams with a description of each dream, gave the diagnosis as being 'good' or 'bad' (written in red), followed by an interpretation of its meaning. One example is:

"if a man sees himself in a dream with

his bed catching fire, bad; it means

driving away his wife."

MAGIC INGREDIENTS

The ingredients used for magical potions were taken from everything around them; human, animal, mineral and plant. They used animal or human excrement and urine, blood, milk and saliva. Mother's milk was always used for good, but saliva could be used in either a healing or a harming spell. Nail and hair clippings were a particularly potent magical addition and herbs and incense were used to attract the presence of the gods with their lovely perfume.

Clay, fat and wax were used to create figures representing animals and people which looked and felt real, imitating the Creator Gods, and therefore making the magic more powerful. In the Louvre Museum is a terracotta model of a woman from the Egyptian Roman period with iron nails through her genitals, chest and head, similar in style to the voodoo dolls seen in West Africa and the Caribbean. The natural assumption is that someone wanted a woman to be maimed or killed, but written sources suggest that it was probably part of a love charm to stop the woman thinking of anyone other than her current lover.

MAGIC SPELLS
One prescription to attract the spirits into the 'magic' circle was:
> *'you put a frog's head on the brazier, then they speak.'*

When the magician had asked all his questions and he was finished with the session:

> *'you put ape's dung on the brazier, then they all depart to their place, and you utter their spell of dismissal also.'*

Most magic that was practiced was for good reasons; love potions, spells to chase away diseases caused by demons, or potions and amulets to protect the young and vulnerable. However, not everyone had good intentions towards their neighbours! This potion was to kill a man:

> *"You put camel's blood with the blood*
>
> *of a dead man into the wine;*
>
> *you make the man drink it; then he dies."*

Another, meant to harm rather than kill:

> *"You put a night-jar's blood into his eye;*
>
> *then he is blinded."*

MEDICINE

We have examined some aspects of magic, now let us look at how they treated their sick and injured with medicine.

Most of the medicinal cures were a mixture of practical treatments, which were believed to either cure the problem or at least alleviate the symptoms, combined with magical words and rituals. Our knowledge of all their treatments comes from more than ten medical papyri that detail ailments and injuries and how they should be treated. The oldest is the *Kahun Medical Papyrus* (*c.*1800 BC) which deals with womens' health, fertility, pregnancy and gynaecological problems. Another is the *Edwin Smith Surgical Papyrus* (*c.*1500 BC) which describes the physical examination, diagnosis, and prognosis of trauma injuries and appropriate surgery. The *London Medical Papyrus* (*c.*1300 BC) and the *Ebers Papyrus* (*c.*1550 BC) both deal with more general problems such as skin infections, eye complaints, burns and bleeding.

THE DOCTOR

From the medical papyri we learn that the Ancient Egyptians knew how to close wounds with stitches, prevent infection with honey, use bandages, splints and poultices and immobilise the head for spinal cord injuries. The procedures in these papyri demonstrate a level of knowledge of medicines that surpassed, in some cases, that of the ancient Greek physician Hippocrates, who lived 1000 years later.

The doctor made his diagnoses through careful observation which involved taking a pulse and looking at, touching and smelling the patient. He then divided the patient's condition into one of three types: those he could treat confidently such as a cleanly broken arm, those he would struggle to cure such as a gaping head wound, and those he declared untreatable such as heart disease. Until quite recently it was believed that cancer was a modern disease, brought on by our lifestyles, food and general pollutants that were not around in ancient times. However, the invention of CT scanning has enabled Egyptologists to undertake new studies of the mummies that have been discovered over the years, which proves that they too suffered from cancer. The medical papyrus details the method of diagnosis:

"you examine a man having tumours on his breast, (and) you find that swelling has spread over his breast; if you put your hand upon his breast upon these tumours, (and) you find them very cool, there being no fever at all when your hand touches him; they have no granulation, they form no fluid, they do not generate secretions of fluid, and they are bulging to your hand.

Treatment: There is no treatment."

PRESCRIPTIONS

Most of the elements of medical prescriptions were not such a witch's brew as those used for magic. Several ingredients they used are known to work: willow leaves (the original source of aspirin) killed pain and were used to decrease the likelihood of infection. Mouldy bread, which is known to contain antibiotics, was used as a poultice, and they applied honey to wounds to keep them disease free. Modern medical practice has re-adopted the use of honey which is well known for its healing properties.

Beer, milk, water, oil and honey were used as the medium to hold together the active ingredients of plants and herbs, minerals such as copper, sulphur and salt and body parts of animals or humans. The most popular animals for medicinal use seem to have been the ass and the cow but prescriptions also detail the need for excrement, blood, feathers, bones etc. from numerous other creatures. To treat minor ailments such as scorpion stings, burns and headaches the doctor would also recite a magic spell. However, simple surgery and the setting of bones do not seem to have ever needed a magical incantation.

MINOR AILMENTS

According to the *Ebers Papyrus,* a simple remedy for burns required *"barley bread, fat and salt, mixed into one. Bandage with it often to make him well"*. Headaches were a common ailment and there are twelve recorded remedies including a poultice of *"fruit of coriander made into a mass, honey is mixed with it, the head is bandaged therewith so that it goes immediately well with him"*.

One thing we all suffer from at some time is indigestion, especially when we have been celebrating and we are prone to eat and drink more than usual. The Ancient Egyptian remedy was to cook onions in sweet beer and drink the cooking liquid for four days. I believe, however, that onions cause heartburn in lots of people so I am very doubtful that this particular remedy actually worked. Could the beer have been the cure?

FERTILITY

It was considered important in Ancient Egypt to have as many children as possible. The child mortality rate was high with large numbers of children not surviving their fourth birthday. Mothers weaned their children at age three; this then exposed them to all the region's illnesses and diseases. Parents needed some of their children to reach adulthood so that the children could take on the task of looking after them in their old age. People were considered elderly at thirty-five (if they had survived that long) and in general pensions were not available. Special state employees such as those who worked on the royal tombs at Deir el-Medina had a privileged position and as such were paid a pension, as were their widows. However, they were not given sufficient to live on and still needed the support of their families. Despite the need for many children, there were aids to contraception in the form of different types of pessaries, including one that contained acacia tip, honey and crocodile dung. This contraceptive might have given the required outcome since acacia tips contain arabic gum which is a spermicide and fresh dung is also believed to be spermicidal. The honey would have glued the mixture together, not caused any harm and effectively formed an impenetrable covering of the cervix. The *London Papyrus* gives this advice "*to cause a woman to love her husband: pods of acacia, pound with honey, anoint your phallus with it and lie with the woman*'; very similar ingredients to the contraceptive!

PREGNANCY

When a woman suspected she was pregnant and needed confirmation she would consult the doctor. He would check the colour of her skin and the condition of her breasts and then test her urine; in a sense, very similar to what happens today. However, their urine test was quite different to what would-be mothers do today; the Ancient Egyptian woman urinated on grains of barley and emmer for a week and if the grains germinated, she was pregnant. There is some scientific evidence that this actually worked. If barley sprouted first the child would be a boy and if the emmer seeds germinated first it meant a baby girl (no scientific evidence!)

BABIES

Within the medical papyri, there was advice for new mothers. It is well known that new babies sometimes cry rather a lot without any obvious reason which is very disconcerting for new parents. The Egyptians' remedy was to mix "*pods of the poppy plant (opium) with fly dirt which is on the wall, make it into one, strain, and give for four days. It acts at once".*

THE DENTIST

There are records of more than one hundred doctors but only seven also held the title of dentist. Their role was to deal with the symptoms of dental problems and was not in any way preventative. The Egyptians generally suffered from extreme tooth wear caused mainly by the sand in the flour they had ground and used for their staple diet of bread and beer, although there was a general belief that toothache was caused by worms. In some mummies that have been examined, the enamel was completely eroded, exposing the soft inner dental pulp, which would have led to large and very painful abscesses. Patients were treated with painkillers such as willow or cloves and the dentist would cut out the poison, aware the infection would come back if he did not clear it out completely.

SURGERY

Surgery was carried out in ancient times, but like here in the UK right up until the 19th century, there was no true anaesthetic. To put their patients to sleep throughout the procedures, the surgeon would give them enough alcohol to drink, or administer opium or mandrake-soaked sponges to keep them asleep. Mandrake is a plant of the nightshade family and highly poisonous; in fact the only part of the plant that is not deadly is the fruit. The root resembles the human body and has been used for centuries in magic and witchcraft by many different cultures. According to legend, the roots scream when they are pulled out of the soil and anyone who hears the scream will die. A solution, according to the scholar Josephus of Jerusalem (*c*.37-100 AD), was to tie a dog to the plant and then walk away. The dog would try to follow you and pull up the roots; the dog would hear the scream and die and then you could safely pick up the mandrake. The Egyptians boiled the root and gave the liquid to patients to send them to sleep while the surgeon operated.

Figure 57 Medical Instruments

Their medical instruments were quite crude but, when finely honed, were not much different to surgical instruments today. They seem to have been mostly knives and tweezers of various sizes and reasonably effective. The surgeon heated the instruments in a fire before using them, which would sterilise them and cauterize the wound, reducing the risk as much as possible of a fatal infection.

This scene is from the tomb of the vizier Ankhmahor at Saqqara dated *c.*2300 BC showing two boys being circumcised; the boy on the left is being cut and the one on the right is possibly having ointment applied to soothe and heal. Circumcision was carried out

Figure 58 Circumcision of Boys

when boys were about 14 years old but it was not practiced at all times; it seems that at certain periods it was undertaken for cleanliness or religious purposes, and at other times not at all. The Romans brought in a ban on the procedure from which only priests were exempt. There is no evidence of female circumcision.

Like many other ancient civilisations, the Egyptians performed cranial surgery, otherwise known as trepanation. It was generally carried out to relieve pressure after a head injury, cure severe headaches and for mental illness. Recovery rates appear to have been satisfactory since some skulls show evidence of good healing with patients living for years after the operation.

We do not have any evidence of plastic surgery but they did have false 'bits and pieces.' A prosthetic toe made from leather and wood, and dated to c.1000 BC was found on the mummified remains of a noblewoman aged 50-60. It has three joints and shows signs of wear indicating that she had worn it while alive; it had not been put on after death for ritual cosmetic reasons. Her natural toe had been amputated and showed signs of good healing.

.

9   THE PYRAMIDS

What were they for? How were they built?

Who built them?

The earliest kings of Egypt, their families and noblemen, were buried in enormous *mastabas* (an Arabic word for 'bench'). The superstructure was of mud-brick, slope-sided and with a flat roof, often nearly 100 m long by 75 m broad and 9 m in height. Within the *mastaba,* above ground level, were a chapel for offerings to the spirit of the deceased and a niche for a statue of the tomb owner. The burial chamber and storeroom for the funerary goods were cut deep into the bedrock and lined with bricks or timber.

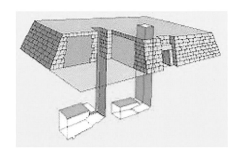

Figure 59 Mastaba

The reason for *mastabas*, and later the pyramids, was threefold and all were related to the religious beliefs of the Egyptians. First, it was a burial place where the deceased could lie in eternal peace, protected from any disturbance and surrounded by family and courtiers who were buried nearby in their own *mastabas*. Second, it provided an area where offerings of food and drink could be made which would provide sustenance for the spirit of the deceased in the Afterlife. This system of offerings continued long after the pharaoh had been laid to rest, maintained by the priesthood as an economic system that employed people and redistributed goods. Third, the shape of the *mastaba* represented the mound of creation that had brought forth every living thing; in their belief system, it was the place where the king would be reborn into the Afterlife. Here, the *ka*, the ba and the body, which had become separated at death, could be transformed into the akh, the eternal spirit of life and light.

The basic method of constructing Egyptian mud bricks was to combine small pieces of straw with soil from the Nile and shape this mixture into bricks by filling wooden moulds with the mud. These were then dried out in the sun and resembled baked clay when they were ready to use. The dry climate of Egypt has partially preserved many of the walls of *mastabas* and other buildings that were constructed in this way.

DEVELOPMENT

The first pharaoh to make the dramatic leap from *mastaba* to pyramid was King Djoser, the first king of the 3rd Dynasty (2667-2648 BC), whose architect Imhotep designed and built the Step Pyramid and its huge temple complex at Saqqara. It was made of quarried stone, not mud-bricks, and as its name suggests it was built

in six gradually decreasing steps up to a height of 60 m. It is regarded as the first large stone building in the world. Instead of the burial chamber being below the surface of the ground in the bedrock, the burial chambers in pyramids were above the ground, deep within the superstructure.

The limestone enclosure wall of the Step Pyramid complex was

Figure 60 Step Pyramid Saqqara

1,645 m long and 10.5 m high and contained an area of fourteen hectares filled with pavilions, chapels, shrines, life-sized statues, buildings and terraces, as well as the standard mortuary and valley temples. Below ground, it was just as remarkable with more than 5.7 km of shafts, tunnels and chambers. The style of columns, statuary and buildings in the enclosure complex at Saqqara became the template for every other pyramid complex that was built over the next one thousand years.

The pharaoh who improved on Djoser's design, changing from a step design to the true straight-sided pyramid, was King Sneferu, first king of the 4th Dynasty (2613-2589 BC), and the greatest pyramid-builder in Egyptian history. He built three colossal pyramids at Meidum and Dashur and a smaller one at Seila.

His first pyramid at Meidum was an eight-step pyramid similar to Djoser's, but the work was abandoned and left incomplete when

Figure 61 The Bent Pyramid

Sneferu moved his court to Dashur. There he built the Bent Pyramid; its slope angle proved too steep (about 74°) and the builders experienced structural problems resulting in collapse and subsidence. This too was abandoned. This was clearly a period of great experimentation as no one yet seems to have had a clear blueprint for the classic straight-sided pyramid.

His next attempt was the Red Pyramid that gets its name from the pink hue of its stone. It was the first successful true pyramid. However, he apparently was still not content and returned to the

Meidum pyramid to transform it into a true, straight-sided pyramid, where it is believed he was buried.

The Pharaoh Sneferu had at least thirteen children, the most famous being King Khufu (also known by the Greek name Cheops). He chose to build his Great Pyramid 40 km north of Dashur on the Giza Plateau. It is the only one remaining of the Seven Wonders of the Ancient World and stands 146 m high – a truly colossal tomb!

THE GREAT PYRAMID

FACTS AND FIGURES

The Great Pyramid of Khufu was the first of three pyramids built at Giza; the others were built by his son Khafre and grandson Menkaure during their respective lifetimes.

One of the reasons the three are still standing while many in other areas have collapsed, is the Giza Plateau on which they are built. It consists of a plate of limestone called the Mokkatan Formation, which is an ideal, regular and strong surface for building. In Figure 62 Khafre's central pyramid (143 m high) looks the tallest when in fact the rightmost pyramid of Khufu is a taller structure (146 m from base to apex) because the section of plateau bearing Khafre's pyramid is 10 m higher than that of Khufu's. The pyramid of Menkaure rises to just 65 m.

Figure 62 Pyramids at Giza

With the construction at Giza, the design of pyramids reached its highest point. The standard features of the pyramid complex, the mortuary and valley temples, were greatly expanded and formalised. The Great Pyramid and its surrounding complex of structures consisted of a causeway, two temples (mortuary and valley), three queens' pyramids, officials' *mastabas* and a small satellite pyramid. These had an estimated combined volume of 2.7 million cu. m, a staggering amount of stone that had to be hewn and placed in position. The Great Pyramid alone contains about 2.3 million blocks of stone. A Turah limestone wall over 8 m high surrounded the finished pyramid and enclosed a 10 m wide courtyard paved in limestone.

The causeway was nearly one kilometre long and linked the valley temple, situated by an offshoot of the Nile, with the mortuary temple next to the pyramid. The body of the pharaoh was delivered by royal barque to the valley temple and then carried along the finely decorated causeway to the mortuary temple. Here, the last rites were performed before its incarceration into the pyramid tomb.

WHO BUILT IT?

Egyptologists and historians have long debated the question of how the Pyramids were built, and standing at the base of the Great Pyramid at Giza it is hard to believe that this enormous monument could have been built by manpower alone. However, all the archaeological evidence (including graffiti left by the work crews on the inside walls) confirms that it was definitely built by humans using the primitive tools which were available to them.

Time and motion studies have estimated that there would have been 2,000 peasant conscripts working at any one time on the pyramid, recruited for three-month stints under the corveé labour system, over twenty years. Corveé or 'unpaid labour' has been used in many societies throughout the world as a means of taxing the population. In Ancient Egypt, all the farmers were required to work on government projects every year when the Nile flooded until it receded. The men worked in the quarries and as labourers building pyramids, temples, canals and roads. For a big project like a pyramid, each man would have worked the four-month inundation season every year and then gone back to his normal work on the farm. This was a non-cash society so they were paid in kind; they were housed, provided with their basic needs and given sufficient food and drink to keep them fit and well.

The work was done by two gangs of 1,000 men, each gang split into five teams of 200 who did the heavy work of rough stone cutting, hauling and placing. Skilled draughtsmen, masons, artisans and craftsmen worked all the year round on the pyramid, as did the slaves, captured during Egypt's conflicts with its neighbouring countries. Another 18-20,000 people supported the building work; carpenters, metalworkers, people to mix the mortar, ramp builders, potters, food makers such as bakers, brewers, food distributors etc.

In recent years, excavations on the workers village near the Giza Pyramids provides archaeological evidence that thousands of workers were housed and well fed while working on the construction of the pyramids at that site. The town is about 400 m south of the sphinx and is now known by its Arabic name, Heit el-Ghurab. Evidence of housing, bakeries, coppersmiths, wine and beer vessels etc. indicate that it was a fully functioning town of many thousands of people. A corral with possible animal slaughter areas and piles of bones has been found on the southern edge of the workers' town. Archaeologists estimate that on average more than 1,800 kg of meat (cattle, sheep and goats) were slaughtered every day to feed the pyramid builders, over three generations.

Researchers have also discovered a nearby cemetery with bodies of pyramid builders; evidence of well-healed bones demonstrates the availability of medical care.

HOW WAS IT BUILT?

MATERIALS

Most of the material used in building the Great Pyramid was limestone that was mined locally, about 300 m from the pyramid site. Gypsum and basalt were taken from the Fayum region, and granite, a non-local stone, was mined in Aswan, 930 km south of Giza. Turah limestone, which is very fine and white, was brought from the east of the Nile and was used as the outer casing of the pyramid; it would have looked quite dazzling in the Egyptian sunshine.

Copper for tools was shipped from Sinai and wood for levers, tracks and sledges, alabaster for statuary and temple pavements, dolerite and quartzite to make tools for pounding and polishing, all had to be brought to the site by ship or road. Fuel for fires to cook food and forge copper tools was not available on the plateau but indigenous trees were harvested from across the Egyptian landscape.

TOOLS

The methods and tools used to build pyramids were not much different to the non-electric tools used by the DIY enthusiast today. The operations needed for its completion involved measuring, aligning, cutting, levering, polishing and so on. The simple tools they used were set squares to get the angles right, a plumb bob suspended from a rod to make vertical adjustments and square levels for levelling the stone surface.

Copper drills used with slurry of water, gypsum and quartz sand were sharp enough to cut the different types of stone, and hand-held dolerite pounders channelled out the granite and basalt blocks in the quarries. Even today, over 4,500 years since Khufu's time, Egyptian masons use hand tools to chip out narrow trenches in limestone to make blocks. Wooden levers or wedges were utilised to detach the stone from the bedrock. Finally, narrow chisels were used to dress and smooth the fine white Turah limestone of the outer casing.

TRANSPORT

Supplies of food and fuel were generally carried on small cargo ships along canals linked to the Nile River, or brought very short distances by road.

A cache of papyri at Wadi el-Jarf on the west bank of the Red Sea near the site of a newly excavated harbour, was recently discovered by archaeologists from the French Institute of Oriental Archaeology led by Pierre Tallet. The cache included a two-month diary written by Merer, an official involved in the building of the Great Pyramid. In it, he details loading his ship with limestone at Turah and copper at Sinai, and taking it for eventual overland transport to the pyramid of Khufu. There were also several trips across the Red Sea of shiploads of food intended to feed the workers at Giza; grain from royal granaries, ribs of beef, fresh figs, bread and beer. The diary included accountants' sheets that detailed the quantities of goods due, deliveries made and the amount still owing.

Huge granite blocks, some weighing 40 tons, had to be brought a distance of over 900 km, all the way down the Nile from Aswan to Giza. Although there are no texts or reliefs narrating specifically how this was done, reliefs on the walls of the causeway of the pyramid of Unas, last ruler of the 5th Dynasty, depict how two large granite columns were moved to his pyramid temples, so we can assume a similar method was used.

The granite columns are shown resting end-to-end on sledges which are raised off the deck of a ship by a support framework of girders, which probably relieved the weight on the deck. When the granite reached Giza, the sledge would have been unloaded and transported to the pyramid site. As nothing would stop the movement of a heavy stone block more quickly than soft desert sand, a road was made from limestone chips and mortar, (the wheel did not arrive in Ancient Egypt until foreign influence introduced the chariot *c.*1600 BC.) Wooden slats like railway sleepers were placed across the roadway and bedded in with more limestone. A thick covering of tafla (desert clay) was laid over the top, which acted as a lubricant; scenes show workers sprinkling water on the mud in front of the sledge, greatly easing its passage. As many men and oxen as were need would have hauled the stones along with ropes.

CONSTRUCTION

The way the pyramids were built has been long forgotten and there are numerous theories regarding how the large blocks of stone were carried from the desert floor right to the top of the pyramid. To raise materials 146 m up the sides of the pyramid must have been a colossal job, and it has been the subject of speculation and experimentation in modern times, as demonstrated by the 1997 NOVA pyramid-building project conducted by Mark Lehner and Roger Hopkins. The accepted conclusion is that a ramp was used but there does not seem to be any agreement on the shape of the ramp; straight-on, spiral, zigzag or a combination. A straight-on

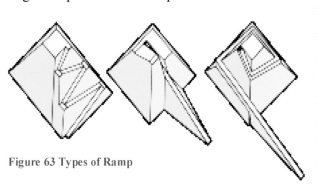

Figure 63 Types of Ramp

ramp would not have been practical, bearing in mind the distance from the quarry to the pyramid, although archaeological evidence from smaller pyramids indicates that this style was sometimes used. The current favourite theory involves spiral ramps round the evolving structure but in the absence of archaeological evidence, other theories should be considered.

One suggestion is that counter-weights were used which would have brought the blocks higher as if in an elevator, the growing pyramid itself used as a ramp. Ropes would be slung across the structure, large buckets at one end, the other end tied to a stone block. The buckets would be filled with sand, acting as a counter-weight to haul up the block.

Another viable theory is that the pyramid was constructed using internal ramps combined with external scaffolding. This theory is based on the premise that the interior of the pyramid was filled with a small number of large blocks, small stones and rubble, all supported by large outer core-casing stones. The corners would have been built first with the central sections left open to allow access to the centre of the pyramid.

Whichever method was really used will remain a mystery but it seems likely that the Ancient Egyptians were innovative builders who used whatever construction method was appropriate for each individual pyramid.

INSIDE THE GREAT PYRAMID
A narrow tunnel leads steeply down from the entrance to the pyramid to a small subterranean chamber carved out of the bedrock. It may have been the original intended burial chamber but it was never completed and was abandoned. A small rough passage leads

from one corner of this chamber, only big enough for one man to crawl along to its dead-end, its purpose unknown.

Within the superstructure is the so-called Queen's Chamber (misnamed by early explorers), a chamber nearly 5 m high that originally housed the *ka* or spirit statue of the king in a large corbelled niche in the east wall. A narrow, cramped ascending passage leads to the magnificent Grand Gallery whose corbelled roof soars to over 8 m. Along its walls are regularly spaced sockets

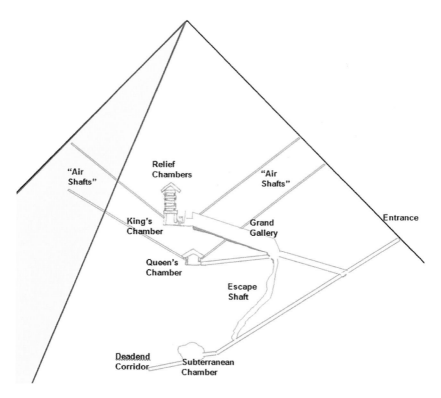

Figure 64 Inside the Great Pyramid

for large wooden beams, believed to have held back the stone blocks that sealed the ascending passage when the builders left. At the end of the Grand Gallery a small antechamber leads into the king's burial chamber.

The King's Chamber still contains the red granite sarcophagus of King Khufu, broken at the corner where robbers had prised it open. The chamber itself is quite magnificent, its walls lined with red granite blocks; it measures 10.5 m x 5.2 m and it is 5.8 m high. Nine granite beams span the ceiling, each estimated to weigh between 25 and 40 tons. It was the first time the Egyptians had spanned such a wide space in stone.

Above the King's Chamber are five stress-relieving chambers, each with the same floor area as the chamber below, designed to distribute the weight and stresses of the tons of stone pressing down from the top. Two narrow shafts, each 20 cm.sq. lead like antennae from both the Queen's and King's Chambers and were probably there to allow the king's spirit to leave the pyramid for its ascent to the gods. In modern times, a robot with video camera was sent up the southern shaft of the Queen's Chamber but it came to a stop after 65 m, the shaft plugged with limestone embedded with two copper pins. Investigations stopped at this point and the meaning of the block, the copper pins and what, if anything, lies beyond, remains a mystery.

When the priests and workmen left the King's Burial Chamber for the last time, they sealed the tomb. Three portcullis stone slabs were dropped down slots in the wall of the antechamber and then huge granite slabs were released from the wooden beams holding them in the Grand Gallery. The slabs of stone slid down to the ascending passage and blocked it. The men would have made their escape through the service shaft before sealing the entrance with limestone in the vain hope that tomb robbers would not be able to identify the entrance.

THE PYRAMID COMPLEX

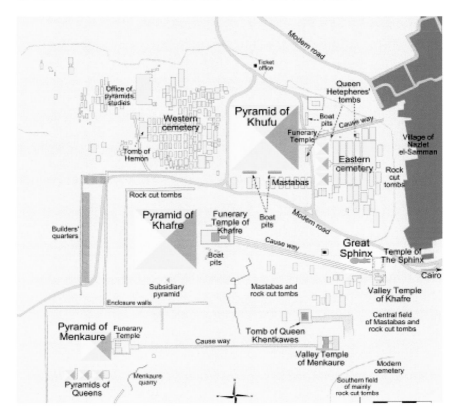

Figure 65 Giza Pyramids Complex

A Turah limestone wall over 8 m high surrounded the pyramid and enclosed a paved courtyard. Beyond that, the complex of Khufu's Great Pyramid contains the usual features of temples and causeway but also features queens' pyramids, cemeteries of *mastabas* for his courtiers and unique boat pits.

TEMPLES

Just outside the Great Pyramid stood the mortuary temple of Khufu, its walls covered in fine relief carvings. This was where offerings could be made to the deceased king and his *ka* spirit, now regarded

101

as an immortal god, and in need of sustenance in the Afterlife. It was larger than any other that had gone before and its walls were of fine limestone carved in relief. The remains of a black basalt open courtyard in front of the temple give an indication of how exceptional it was.

The valley temple, of which only a small amount of basalt pavement remains, was the reception area for the body of the king when it was brought by boat to the tomb site. Linking both temples was a causeway nearly one kilometre long with high, finely carved walls through which the body of the pharaoh was carried on his final earthly journey.

QUEENS' PYRAMIDS

Within the complex Khufu built three pyramids for queens, each about one-fifth the size of his own. All three have a passage that slopes down to a chamber cut out of the bedrock and is lined with masonry.

For whom they were meant remains a mystery. It is believed that one may have been for Hetepheres, thought to be Khufu's mother. A deep shaft 28 m away from the pyramid and leading to a small chamber, contained a beautiful alabaster sarcophagus and canopic jars as well as broken pottery and furniture. It seems to have been the reburial place of Hetepheres, her original tomb having been disturbed. Another of the pyramids may have been for a queen Henutsen of whom we know little. The other pyramid might belong to a queen Meritetes based on inscriptions that have been found. All three had mortuary chapels (smaller versions of Khufu's mortuary temple).

BOAT PITS

Five boat shaped pits and two rectangular pits have been discovered in the vicinity of the Great Pyramid. The two southern rectangular pits, discovered in 1954, each had a roof of limestone slabs. The slabs were raised from one pit revealing a completely dismantled, full-size boat of 1,224 separate parts. Made from cedar wood, many of the parts had U-shaped holes so that the boat could be tied together with ropes made from vegetable fibres. The boat was gradually reassembled and measures over 43 m. (See page 124 Khufu's Royal Barque.) It is now housed in its own museum next to the Great Pyramid. A second deconstructed boat was found and is currently being rebuilt; when finished it will be displayed in the same museum.

It is believed that this boat was related to Khufu's final voyage to his pyramid. Items linked to royal burials were considered very special and highly charged with the power of the king and the gods. To neutralise them they were dismantled and buried separately, close to the pharaoh but outside the immediate burial area.

THE GREAT SPHINX
So far we have looked at the pyramid complex of Khufu, but we will now turn our attention to something that was built for his son Khafre.

Figure 66 The Great Sphinx

This truly colossal piece of sculpture, situated at the end of Khafre's causeway near the Valley Temple, is carved from the natural limestone bedrock and towers 20 m into the sky. It is 73 m long and 19 m wide. It has a human head and the body of a lion, a standard form associated with royalty. The royal human head on the body of a lion symbolised the strength and power of the lion controlled by the intelligence of the pharaoh. The lion's mane has been replaced by a nemes headdress which was exclusive to Egyptian kings. Sketches made in 1757 show that the nose of the Sphinx was missing i.e. prior to the arrival in Egypt of Napoleon's army who were thought to have damaged it, but it is now believed to have been chiselled off in ancient times. The Sphinx probably also had a 'false beard', symbol of the pharaoh's divinity, which is also missing from the statue.

The Sphinx became buried up to its shoulders in sand after the Giza Necropolis was abandoned. The first documented attempt at an excavation dates to c.1400 BC, when Thutmose IV's workmen managed to dig out the front paws, between which he built a small open-air chapel containing a granite slab, known as the Dream Stela. On it he commemorates his accession to the throne and how as a young prince he fell asleep in the shadow of the statues head (the rest of the sphinx was covered with sand). The god Khepri-Re-Atum appeared to him in a dream and offered him the throne of Upper and Lower Egypt in return for repairing the sphinx and clearing the sand. The work was done and he did become pharaoh.

Modern excavations by Giovanni Caviglia in 1817 uncovered the Sphinx's chest and the entire statue was finally excavated by 1936, in digs led by Émile Baraize. Since then the Egyptian government have repaired its head and neck, damaged due to erosion.

MODERN PYRAMIDS

Since archaeologists re-discovered them, the western world has been fascinated by pyramids, believing they have a 'magical' quality. A new revival in the late 20th century AD has resulted in many more being erected. They have not been built for the dead as in ancient times, but are meant to house the living.

The best-known pyramid house is in Illinois, USA and stands six storeys high. It is completely gilded in 24ct gold, including its pyramid shaped outhouses. Inside there are stone walls and floors to simulate the inside of a tomb, all decorated with figures and hieroglyphic script. Pyramid shaped rooms and fireplaces, statues of gods and other paraphernalia, complete the Ancient Egyptian décor.

Figure 67 Gold Pyramid Illinois USA

In the Sonoran Desert of Arizona, a white pyramid house stands 13 m tall, its guest room complete with sarcophagus in which visitors can lie and gaze at the stars through two triangular windows.

Many organisations in the USA have chosen a pyramid design; the Rainforest Pyramid in Texas is 38 m tall and houses the worlds largest indoor rainforest and California State University has a 105 m tall Physical Education Pyramid to name just two. In Europe, there is a glass pyramid outside the Louvre, France and pyramids were common grave markers in the 19th century in England, particularly in Highgate Cemetery, London.

HEALING POWERS?

Do pyramids have special powers?

Some people believe that blunt razor blades and knives placed under a pyramid become sharp again, and that food does not go off, dry up or rot. It is also believed that sitting under a pyramid shape will heal both the body and the mind while generating feelings of peace and harmony. Many companies make good profits by selling pyramid shaped boxes and tents, but their benefits have never been scientifically proven.

10   THE TOMB BUILDERS

Innovative, Creative & Industrious

In Egypt's early dynastic history, royalty and the elite were buried in *mastabas* and pyramids, huge structures that dominated the skyline. Unfortunately, because they were so highly visible, they were the target of tomb robbers who broke through the defence systems set up by the builders, and they took everything that was inside them. In response to this on-going threat, Thutmosis I, third pharaoh of the New Kingdom, decided to have 'invisible' tombs built on the west bank of the Nile opposite his capital Thebes. This site was chosen for several reasons; the quality of its limestone rock, its close proximity to Thebes, its steep cliffs which made it easy to protect, and the pyramid-shaped top of the large mountain, Al-Qurn, which is visible from the valley.

The best skilled artisans in the country were employed to cut and decorate the royal tombs in the Valley of the Kings, the pharaohs' burial site for the next 450 years. The workers and their families were housed in a village named *Set Maat* or The Place of Truth, now called Deir el-Medina.

DEIR EL-MEDINA

Situated in a desert valley within walking distance of the Valley of the Kings, the village of Deir el-Medina had 68 small mud-brick terraced houses. One narrow road ran through its centre and it was surrounded by a stone wall, not quite thick or strong enough to protect the villagers from serious threat but enough to deter strangers from entering. It is believed that some workmen stayed overnight nearer to the tombs; shed-like buildings have been found which were used to store excavation tools, copper carving implements, plaster, oil, paints etc. and may have been slept in by workmen too tired to trudge home at the end of the day. Sentries were posted near the site at all times to guard the tools and to ensure no outsiders knew the whereabouts of the royal tombs.

The houses varied in size and form but all had the same general layout of one room leading into another, providing sufficient space and privacy for a family of ten. The houses ranged in size from 40-120 sq.m with the average about 70 sq.m The outside walls were painted white and the inner walls were often covered in multi-

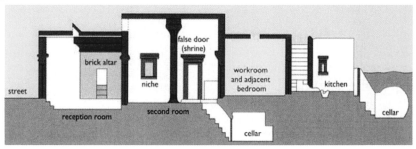

Figure 68 Typical House Deir el-Medina

coloured decorations. The outer wooden door was usually painted red to ward off evil. Cellars were dug under the house and near the open-air kitchen to keep food and drink cool and fresh. Probably the favourite place for the adults during the summer months was the roof, accessible by a set of steps leading up from the kitchen. This area would offer some cooling breezes after the heat of the day and a chance to socialise with neighbours.

THE GREAT PIT

Just outside the village, there is a huge pit, 50 m deep and 30 m wide with a rock-cut staircase spiralling down to the bottom.

Deir el-Medina lies within a desert region with no water readily available and twice during the life of the village unsuccessful attempts were made to dig down to the water table. Work was abandoned over the course of the years and the enormous crater was gradually filled with village debris, including hundreds of pieces of ostraca, the richest source of information we have about village life. Unusually for those times, there was a high level of literacy in the village, reaching a peak of at least 40% of the villagers in the 20th Dynasty compared to 3-4% in the average population. The Deir el-Medina site is unique because of the thousands of written records that were recovered. A huge variety of texts were found in the Great Pit; there were shopping lists, laundry lists, magic spells, doctors prescriptions and private letters. The villagers also wrote on papyri, some of which has survived in the form of administrative records that were found in the official village archives and the private library of the scribe Qenherkhepeshef. They were just as varied, with records of economic transactions, complaints put into the local court and details of the verdicts reached, as well as poems and stories. In fact, everything that we write or need to record today, they did too. Some ostraca have drawings and sketches showing they had a good eye for detail and a sense of humour.

SUPPLIES

In this cashless society, the workers were paid in kind by the state who supplied them with food, fuel and clothing. Their basic salary was a monthly grain ration of four sacks (*c*.300 litres) of emmer wheat and barley to make their staple diet of bread and beer. It has been estimated that this was more than sufficient to feed a family of ten, with enough surplus to barter for other goods. In addition, they received a regular quota of fish, vegetables, firewood and water. Clothes, oil and meat were given much less regularly and were regarded as luxury items. Higher-ranking villagers such as the chief workman, draughtsmen and scribes were given larger quotas than the lower ranks of stonecutters and plasterers.

In the latter part of the 20th Dynasty, the ration deliveries became irregular and incomplete. A detailed journal known as the Turin Strike Papyrus records protest demonstrations by the villagers, angry with the government over the extended periods of shortages they had been subject to under the rule of Rameses III. Coincidentally, records of the ration deliveries for that period are still preserved and confirm that the villagers had been living on very short rations and were justifiably upset.

The state also supplied the villagers with laundrymen who collected their soiled laundry and took it to the riverbank where they washed it with natron and water. Some clothing that was recovered from Deir el-Medina still bears the laundry marks and a few records survive of the washing that had been sent out and returned. Servants were supplied by the state and were detailed to help with the household chores, usually turning the monthly grain ration into flour and helping with bread and beer making.

The workmen of Deir el-Medina were highly regarded and, as such, their supplies from the state were generous. However, not surprisingly, the standard issue did not always satisfy individual tastes and there was a great deal of trading between households. Men made furniture and funerary goods in their spare time and women made clothes, all of which found eager buyers in the village. Although there was no cash, each item was given a value or price measured in the equivalent weight/value of grain, copper or silver called a *deben*, although copper and silver rarely changed hands.

For instance, a box valued at ten copper *deben* could be exchanged for two tunics worth five copper *deben* each. Surplus commodities that had been made in the village, or rations that were not needed, could also be traded at the local market that was held at the riverbank. Here they could barter their goods for items they wanted such as pots, jewellery and utensils.

THE WORKMEN

Whenever a pharaoh died, one of the main priorities of his successor was to commission his own burial tomb. Most of them were large and took years to complete; the tomb of Rameses II, KV 7 is one of the largest and covers 686 sq.m extending 168 m into the hillside. It has four corridors, a pillared chamber, an antechamber, burial chamber and eleven side chambers as well as stairs. In common with all royal tombs it is rich in imagery, depicting the magical passage of the king through the Underworld to the Afterlife. The figures are cut in raised relief i.e the finished design is higher than the surrounding surface, and are painted in a glorious palette of rich and vibrant colour. The people who achieved it all were the workmen of Deir el-Medina.

Once the vizier and other court officials had chosen the site of the tomb for the new pharaoh the working gangs set to work. There were two gangs of 16-24 men each – one gang to work down the left side of the tomb and the other the right side. Both gangs had an overseer and a full complement of each type of specialist needed to complete the work. They had a working week of eight days followed by two rest days.

Starting with a blank cliff-face, the stonecutters hollowed out the limestone corridors and chambers of the tomb with hand axes made from chert (a sharp edged sedimentary rock), copper chisels and dolerite pounders, and carpenters built wooden scaffolding to enable them to open out the upper sections. The walls were left smooth to allow the plasterers to cover them with gypsum and whitewash ready for decoration.

The preliminary drawings were marked in outline on the walls by the draughtsmen and then carved in raised relief by the sculptor. Adjustments were made and the final reliefs were painted, the artist adding detail as he went to enhance the images. The basic colours they used were red, blue, green, yellow, black and white which the painter mixed with gum to help bind the colour to the walls. Red and yellow were obtained by grinding ochre, blue could be azurite or blue frit (a quartz, lime and copper compound also known as Egyptian blue), and green came from various natural materials including malachite. Black was usually made from soot, and gypsum was used for the colour white. The final stage was for the scribe to write the hieroglyphic script.

The working conditions were hot, humid, dusty and dark and it seems quite miraculous that they produced work of such splendour and fine detail. Daylight did not penetrate very far into the tomb and artificial light would seem to have been barely adequate. Documents from Deir el-Medina record that they had wicks made from waste linen that had been twisted and soaked in oil or fat with the addition of salt. This was a specially adapted source of light since the common lamps used in ancient times produced a smoky flame, and there are no soot deposits on the ceilings of the tombs.

THE WOMEN

While the men of the village toiled away in the bowels of the earth, the women had a completely different life-style. Their role was to bear children, and to look after them and the household, cleaning, cooking and making beer. Any spare time was taken up with weaving and making clothes for the use of the family or to trade.

They supported each other as midwives, nurses and hairdressers, and did community work as songstresses at the local temple, and jurors in the village law court.

The women of Deir el-Medina were not employed in paid work and so were not financially independent, relying on their fathers and husbands for support. The houses in the village were tied to the jobs so when a worker died his house was taken over by his successor and his family had to find alternative accommodation. A woman would then have depended on the charity of family and friends to house and support her (and any young children). It is well recorded that the women of Deir el-Medina seem to have inherited many more sheds and storehouses than were left to men, possibly as somewhere to live if there was nowhere else.

Figure 69 Women in the Temple

Women did have legal rights; men and women inherited equally from their parents and any property that a woman brought into a marriage remained her own even when the marriage ended in divorce, as well as one-third of the wealth the couple had acquired while they were together. In general, women were not able to generate wealth for themselves although some did have substantial assets, a combination of funds from selling goods they had made, and property inherited from parents and husband who had pre-deceased them.

THE TOMBS

A total of 63 tombs and 2 unexcavated tomb entrances have been discovered in the Valley of the Kings with possibly many more still to be found. On the hillside to the west of the village, the workers also built tombs for themselves.

Apart from size and splendour, the main difference between a villager's tomb and that of a pharaoh was visibility – the workers did not hide their tombs. They were each topped by a small pyramid, no more than 10 m high, that contained a small chapel chamber. In front, there was a forecourt surrounded by a mud-brick wall that enclosed a garden or pond. Spaces being at a premium here, the tombs were crowded along the hillside, each tomb used by an entire family for several generations.

The decoration of the tombs also sets them apart; other private, non-royal tombs in Egypt are decorated with scenes from the owner's daily life, banquets, processions and their funerary ceremonies. Here, the villagers have aligned themselves very closely with royalty, depicting scenes and texts from the *Book of the Dead* which had once been restricted to royal tombs, possibly a way of claiming a special relationship between themselves, the pharaoh and the gods.

No two royal tombs in the Valley are alike although they all had the important constituent parts of burial chamber, a tomb statue representing the deceased, a side chamber for burial goods, a chapel where offerings could be made and a 'false door' through which the spirit (*ka*) of the deceased could come to partake of the offerings. The decoration, size and layout of the tombs reflected the changing explanations of life after death developed by the priests. The earliest

18th Dynasty tombs were relatively small and cut into the base of steep cliffs to ensure the entrances were hidden by falling debris brought down by heavy rains. The tombs of the 19th Dynasty were slightly larger but by the 20th Dynasty they were huge with a series of long, wide corridors and numerous high chambers.

Here I will highlight a few of the tombs they built for themselves and for royalty to demonstrate their expert craftsmanship.

WORKERS TOMBS

TT1: THE TOMB OF SENNEDJEM

All we know of Sennedjem is that he was a senior official in Deir el-Medina. His tomb was discovered undisturbed in 1886, and the artefacts were distributed all around the world before any proper study was made; information on him was lost. He was buried along with his wife, Iy-neferti, and their family.

Figure 70 Cat of Heliopolis

Almost all of the decorations within the tomb, painted on a vivid background of yellow ochre, are perfectly preserved, and considered some of the most beautiful within the cemetery. This scene depicts the solar cat of Heliopolis sitting beneath a persea tree and slashing with a knife the evil serpent Apophis, enemy of the sun god, leaving it dripping with blood.

This scene is one of the best-known and favourite tomb scenes from the New Kingdom. The full scene is in four registers and shows Sennedjem and his wife ploughing and bringing in the harvest in the Afterlife. It is a standard illustration that accompanies Chapter 110 from the *Book of the Dead*, but this is the most beautifully executed of all similar drawings.

Figure 71 Sennedjem & Wife Harvesting

TT3: THE TOMB OF PASHEDU

Pashedu lived in Deir el-Medina during the reigns of Sety I and Rameses II, working as a stonemason responsible for digging the royal tombs, creating corridors, chambers and pillared halls. It was discovered in 1834 during illicit digging but visited later by Robert Hay, a Scottish artist, who recorded in detail the beautifully decorated walls.

Twenty-nine steps descend into the bedrock leading to a small antechamber and a single vaulted corridor leads to the burial chamber. Here a scene depicts Pashedu crouching by a stream in the shade of a palm tree laden with clusters of dates. Chapter 12 of the *Book of the Dead* describes how the water under the tree will quench the fires of the Underworld and so protect the deceased from harm.

Above the doorway leading into the burial chamber, a scene is of the god Ptah-Sokar-Osiris in the form of a falcon. Its wings are finely detailed (but of unequal size), spreading out beneath a *wedjat*-eye. The falcon is sitting on a simple boat and before him kneels Kaha, one of Pashedu's sons, offering praise to the god.

The scene depicted on the rear wall of the burial chamber is of Osiris sitting on a throne, holding a crook and flail. A god seated in front of Osiris presents a bowl with burning tapers and behind him, a *wedjat*-eye with arms also offers up a bowl of tapers. Pashedu kneels below in a pose of adoration while the Horus falcon looks on.

Elsewhere in the tomb are figures of all of Pashedu's family including his sons, parents and granddaughter, his wife and her parents and extended family, all in various poses of adoration of the gods or honouring their parents. The women of the family are elegantly dressed in elaborately pleated dresses and perfectly coiffed long hair.

ROYAL TOMBS
KV 34: THE TOMB OF THUTMOSE III

Thutmose III was the fifth king of the 18th Dynasty, so one of the first pharaohs to be buried in the Valley of the Kings. It was discovered in 1898 and had been plundered in ancient times. However, the sarcophagus of the pharaoh was still in the burial chamber together with some funerary items including several wooden statues of the king and various deities, pieces of wooden model boats, pottery, and bones from a baboon and a bull.

Figure 72 Oval tomb and Sarcophagus

In these early tombs, only a few of the

117

chambers were decorated and some of the walls are not even smoothed with plaster. Instead of scenes from the *Book of the Dead*, the texts and paintings are from the *Imydwat* or the *Book of the Secret Chamber* that gives an hour-by-hour account of the nightly journey of the sun through the Underworld. The emphasis on the *Imydwat* in royal tombs continued until the end of the 18th Dynasty.

The tomb of Thutmose III is cut high into the cliffs, 20 m above the valley floor. Steps and ramps lead steeply down into the tomb through un-plastered and undecorated corridors, until eventually, at the third chamber, the ceiling is beautifully decorated. The background is dark blue to resemble the sky and it is littered with bright yellow stars, a theme which is continued in the large, oval burial chamber that is more than 14 m by 8.5 m.

The walls of the burial chamber are decorated with scenes from the *Imydwat,* drawn in black and red on a pale yellow background to mimic text written on papyrus. The figures are stick-like and the hieroglyphs are done in a cursive style, very different from the formalised text and life-like scenes in later tombs.

Figure 73 Detail from tomb of Thutmose III

KV 9: THE TOMB OF RAMESES VI

Shortly after Rameses VI burial in 1136 BC grave robbers plundered his tomb. His remains were re-buried and were found in 1898 in KV35, the tomb of Amenhotep II. A medical examination revealed that his head, hands and feet had been broken into several pieces by an axe, probably wielded by the tomb robbers to recover his jewellery.

His tomb is one of the most impressive in the Valley of the Kings and one of the six largest with very wide corridors, high ceilings and pillared halls.

It is 117 m long and covers 510 sq.m It is decorated in vivid colours against a crisp white background that makes it fresh and bright. There is a significant emphasis on the sun god Ra in the

Figure 74 Detail from tomb of Rameses VI

decorations, which come from the *Book of Gates*, the *Book of Caverns* and the *Books of the Sky*, all texts related to the journey of the deceased through the Underworld. The *Book of the Earth* appears for the first time in this tomb in the spectacularly decorated burial chamber.

The burial chamber is covered from floor to ceiling in highly coloured decorative images on a white background. (Figure 74) The ceiling in the chamber is in stark contrast, being an astronomical themed ceiling of yellow against a black sky, depicting the journey of the sun through the Underworld with the sky goddess Nut extending across the whole length of the ceiling.

The work done by the talented workmen of Deir el-Medina is a delight to see; if you ever go into the tombs in the Valley of the Kings that they created from nothing, spare a thought for the men who carved them out of the rock and then decorated them so beautifully over 3,000 years ago.

To finish this chapter, I would like to show you one of my favourite Egyptian drawings. It is a satirical sketch on papyrus depicting two 'servant' cats waiting on their 'mistress', a mouse. The elegant lady mouse is having her hair done by a cat maid while other cat servants offer food and drink. It could have been an illustration from a children's story but mice are occasionally portrayed as officials ordering cats around. Perhaps this is the equivalent of political cartoons representing popular feelings about the ruling classes, the government and officialdom in general.

Figure 75 Cats attending a Mouse

11   TREASURES OF ANCIENT EGYPT

Wonders to Behold!

There are thousands of ancient artefacts and monuments that have been discovered in Egypt that can be regarded as treasure, from the wonderful jewellery worn by Tutankhamun to temples and shrines at numerous religious sites. This chapter will highlight some of them and explain why they are true treasures of the world.

NARMER PALETTE *c.*3100 BC

Named after Narmer, the first king of the 1st Dynasty, the Narmer Palette is a flat, shield shaped plate of dark greeny-grey siltstone – material that is fine grained, hard, does not flake and was quarried at Wadi Hammamet in the Eastern desert. It is about 64 cm in height which suggests that it was a ceremonial palette recording the victories of the king, and not used for practical purposes. It was found by the British archaeologist J.E. Quibell in 1897 at Nekhen (Hierakonpolis), the ancient Pre-dynastic capital in southern Egypt.

Figure 76 Narmer Palette (front)

The top of the palette on both sides has the name of the king inscribed between two bovine heads: they could be of the cow goddess Hathor or may be bulls' heads to imply the bull-like vigour and strength of the king.

The front: In the top scene, Narmer is wearing the Red Crown of Lower Egypt and he is holding a mace in his left hand. He is in a procession of people next to ten decapitated bodies of their enemies, lying on the ground with their heads thrown between their legs. In the central scene, two men are tying together the stretched necks of two incredible animals that may represent the union of Upper and Lower Egypt by King Narmer. The scene at the bottom continues the imagery of conquest and victory. A bull, representing the king, tramples a fallen enemy and attacks the walls of a city with its horns.

The back: Most of the back of the palette is taken up by a finely carved and highly detailed relief of Narmer wearing the White Crown of Upper Egypt. He is in a typically Egyptian 'smiting' pose, ready to strike down a floored enemy who he is holding by the hair. A falcon, symbol of the king, is perched on top of papyrus plants in the top right-hand corner, and appears to be holding a rope that is wrapped around the head of an Asiatic, one of the traditional enemies of Egypt. At the bottom, underneath the king's feet, are two naked enemies being symbolically trampled.

Figure 77 Narmer palette (back)

This shield deserves a place in a list of treasures because it is not only a piece of very fine art which has survived in almost perfect condition for 5,000 years, it is also an amazing historical record (either true or imaginary) of the successful conquests of Ancient Egypt under the governorship of Narmer.

RAHOTEP AND HIS WIFE NOFRET *c.*2600 BC

My next items are a double treasure; limestone statues of Rahotep and his wife Nofret, which were discovered when his *mastaba* at

Meidum was excavated in 1871. Rahotep's origins have not been confirmed but he was definitely a man of high birth and was probably a son of the 4th Dynasty Pharaoh Sneferu. The parents of Nofret are also unknown but they most likely belonged to the royal household.

The statues are in an excellent state of preservation, looking as if

Figure 78 Rahotep & Nofret

they were freshly painted yesterday. The figures are each just over 120 cm high and are seated on high-backed chairs with footrests. The black painted hieroglyphs on the back of Rahotep's chair give his name and titles such as 'Overseer of construction' and 'Vizier'. Unusually for images from Ancient Egypt, Rahotep sports a trimmed black moustache. Nofret wears a shoulder length dark wig but her own hair is visible beneath it.

The truly remarkable thing about both these statues, and the reason I believe they are so special, are the eyes: they are made from rock crystal and look real! The eyes sparkle and glow as if they can see and bring an extraordinary life-like quality to the statues. Egyptian workmen who first opened the tomb saw them in the torch light staring out of the dark tomb and they fled in terror. They are true works of art and Ancient treasures.

KHUFU'S ROYAL BARQUE *c.*2566 BC

On the south side of the Great Pyramid of Khufu at Giza, two boat pits, each covered by a roof of limestone slabs, were discovered in 1954. When the roof was removed from the first pit, it revealed the planking of a great boat that had been completely dismantled but

arranged in a semblance of its finished form. There were 1,224 separate parts made from cedar wood, many with large U-shaped holes so that the planking could be stitched together using ropes made of vegetable fibres. After many years of painstaking restoration work the boat was re-assembled and is now housed in its own museum next to the Great Pyramid; it is 43.3 m long.

Figure 79 Khufu's Royal Barque

It is very likely that this boat was used to bring the deceased pharaoh Khufu to his final resting place within the pyramid. The sophisticated workmanship employed when this craft was originally built is admirable; the prow and stern are in the form of papyrus stalks, imitating perhaps a style of papyrus reed boat that was used in pre-dynastic times. A cabin enclosed within a reed-mat structure with papyrus style poles is on the deck and would have housed the coffin of Khufu on his journey.

The Great Pyramid of Khufu is the last remaining of the Seven Wonders of the Ancient World (see Chapter 9 Pyramids) but this treasure is unique. It is beautifully made from cedar wood, material not found in Egypt, and is testament to the skill of the craftsmen who built this sea-worthy craft more than 4,000 years ago. Its purpose was special too; it was used for the sacred purpose of transporting the remains of a Great Pharaoh.

PRINCESS SITHATHORIUNET PECTORAL c.1880 BC

The Middle Kingdom was the period in Ancient Egyptian history when the peak of their jewellery-making expertise was reached, producing works of refinement and great elegance. This 12th Dynasty pectoral was found at el-Lahun in the shaft tomb of Princess Sithathoriunet, daughter of the pharaoh Senusret II.

The cloisonné pectoral is gold inlaid with 372 carefully cut pieces of semi-precious stones; carnelian, lapis lazuli, turquoise and garnet. The gold necklace on which it hangs has beads of carnelian, lapis lazuli and turquoise feldspar. The chain is 82 cm long and the pectoral is 4.5 cm high and 8.2 cm wide.

Figure 80 Sithathoriunet Pectoral

This piece of jewellery, as with all jewellery worn by royal women, was not only for adornment or for an indication of status. Each part of the design was symbolic of the myths surrounding Egyptian royalty, their magic infusing the wearer with god-like powers that enabled her to support the king in his role as a living god. It features two Horus falcons crowned with sun discs standing on a bar representing the primordial ocean. One claw rests on a *shen* sign (representing eternity) with the other claw supporting two notched palm ribs (hieroglyphic symbol for 'year'). The ribs are held by the god Heh who was the god of infinity. Above this is the cartouche for Senusret II flanked by two supporting royal cobras each holding an *ankh*. Since it was the king who ultimately benefited from the magical powers inherent in the jewellery, it explains why his name, Senusret, rather than that of his daughter the princess, appears in the designs.

It is an exquisite piece of jewellery that artisans these days would find it difficult to match, and it has the added attraction of being steeped in magical symbolism.

THE TEMPLES AT KARNAK

Figure 81 Statues at Karnak

The earliest structures found at Karnak are dated to at least the Middle Kingdom (*c.*2055-1650 BC) but there is evidence that the site was inhabited thousands of years before. What we see today is the result of almost constant building activity that began over 4,700 years ago. Karnak is huge, covering over two square kilometres and its principal building, the Temple of Amen-Ra is the largest religious structure ever built. It is surrounded by enormous temples dedicated to his wife Mut and their son Khonsu, and all of them were renewed, repaired and enlarged by successive pharaohs. Each king seems to have wanted to 'out-do' his predecessor by building bigger and better monuments; over two hundred large structures have been found at the site. Fortunes were spent on building here during the New Kingdom, greatly adding to Karnak's size and complexity and making its priesthood one of the richest in Egypt.

The Karnak site is one of the most awesome places in Egypt, magnificent in its grandeur and vastness, seemingly built for giants with its endless pillars reaching up to the sky.

NEBAMUN TOMB RELIEF c.1350 BC

Nebamun was an Egyptian "scribe and counter of grain" during the New Kingdom c. 1350 BC. The paintings in his tomb were chiselled off the walls and purchased by a collector who then sold them to the British Museum in 1821. The collector died without ever revealing the site of the tomb.

Figure 82 Nebamun 'fishing & fowling'

The scene is one of hunting or 'fishing and fowling in the marshes' as it is popularly known. Nebamun is standing on a light boat and, in perfect balance he holds captured birds in one hand and a throw-stick in the other. Birds are flying up from the papyrus thicket in alarm at his intrusion. Nebamun's wife is dressed in finery as if attending a banquet and their child is sitting in the bottom of the boat under her father's legs. It is an idealised family scene taking place in the Afterlife, and not one likely to have happened during his lifetime, since his wife and child would never normally have accompanied him on a hunting expedition. The hieroglyphic inscription below Nebamun's raised arm explains he is "taking recreation and seeing what is good in the place of eternity."

Every aspect of this scene has been perfectly executed, from the main figures of Nebamun and his family to the natural environment. The exquisitely painted birds are everywhere, numerous types of fish swim under the boat, and beautiful flowers and fluttering butterflies all compete for attention, but together create a harmonious rural scene. The ginger cat is a delight; it has leapt from the bottom of the boat and captured birds in its mouth and claws and looks towards its master for approval.

GLASS FISH c.1345 BC

This 14 cm long multi-coloured glass vessel is in the form of the Nile 'bulti'-fish and was found in a private house at el-Amarna,

buried under a plaster floor together with two glass jugs and some metal objects.

The body is core-built in blue glass, and is decorated with simple

Figure 83 Glass Bulti Fish

ribbons of yellow and white representing scales, with threads of turquoise on the fins. A deep band of yellow outlines the mouth and the eyes are white opaque circles with the pupils represented by black thread loops. Its use is not obvious but it may have been used to store ointment.

It is a very beautiful item and a fine example of the skill and artistry of the ancient glassmaker who produced it.

TUTANKHAMUN'S GOLD COFFIN *c.*1327 BC

The magnificent gold coffin of Tutankhamun symbolises Ancient Egypt in the minds of many people. This solid gold inner coffin

containing his mummy was inside two outer coffins. It measures about 1.88 m in length and weighs over 110 kgs. The metal was beaten from heavy gold sheet, and it is inlaid with semi-precious stones, lapis lazuli and coloured glass.

The image of the pharaoh that was sculpted on this coffin is today oddly spiritual and ghostly, due

Figure 84 Gold Coffin of Tutankhamun

to the decomposition of the calcite whites of the eyes. The pupils are obsidian, while the eyebrows and cosmetic lines are inlaid with blue coloured glass, imitating lapis lazuli. The nemes headdress is pleated in relief and the false beard was made separately and then attached to the finished face.

His ears have piercings to hold earrings (which were worn up to puberty by males) and had patches of thin gold foil concealing the holes when it was found. Around his neck, again made separately and attached before burial, is a falcon collar inlaid with eleven rows of lapis lazuli with beads of semi-precious stones such as carnelian and felspar.

Tutankhamun's arms are shown crossed upon his chest with his signs of office, the crook and flail, held in his hands. The winged goddesses Isis and Nephthys have their wings spread protectively around his body. Two vertical columns of hieroglyphic text run down the front of the coffin lid to the feet, where a figure of Isis is kneeling upon the hieroglyph for 'god' upon the soles of the feet.

The coffin lid was fitted with handles and was attached to its base by means of eight gold tongues, four on each side, which dropped into sockets in the base and were retained by gold pins.

When it was found the coffin did not gleam brightly as it does now; it was covered with a thick black pitch-like layer that extended from the hands down to the ankles. This was actually a fatty resinous perfume which had been poured over the coffin, completely filling the space between it and the base of the second coffin and making them stick firmly together. The removal of this resinous layer was difficult to say the least, according to Howard Carter the archaeologist who discovered the tomb.

There must have been many other pharaohs who were buried with equally splendid treasures, lost through time to tomb robbers and melted down or sold to private collectors, but this treasure of Tutankhamun has survived. It seems unbelievable that craftsmen living over 3,000 yeas ago could fashion such an item of outstanding beauty with expert skill and artistic flair.

12   THE SACRED LANGUAGE

Who discovered the 'key' to hieroglyphics?

Some tips on learning to read it.

The unification of such an extensive tract of land as Egypt was unique and in contrast to the political situations of its neighbours, Nubia, Mesopotamia, and Syria-Palestine. A possible uniting factor was that a common language or dialect was spoken throughout the regions, making it easier for them to communicate and subsequently unite, although it is impossible to know how the language was spoken over 5,000 years ago. Their written language is the second oldest in the world, preceded only by Sumerian from western Asia.

During the pharaonic period the written language passed through several stages. Hieroglyphic text, given its name by the Greeks and meaning 'divine speech' or 'sacred carvings', was the sacred language of Ancient Egypt, since it was only used for religious purposes on monuments, tombs and temples. Hieratic, a cursive version of hieroglyphics, was the language used by the administration for keeping records, sending letters, writing instructions and for literary texts such as stories and poems, but never for religious purposes. It was written on pieces of pottery, wood and papyrus.

By the 25th Dynasty demotic script had emerged and for several centuries it was used side by side with Greek. The third century AD saw the introduction of coptic script which gradually replaced demotic and hieroglyphic scripts; this consisted of the Greek alphabet and six demotic signs, and was introduced for religious and cultural reasons. Coptic survived in the liturgy of the Coptic Church and is still used today, centuries after the emergence of Arabic as the spoken and written language of Egypt. The Egyptian people had become Christian, and the hieroglyphic text and ancient gods were banned as idolatrous. The last known hieroglyphic inscription, found on a temple gateway on the island of Philae, was written in AD 394. Within a generation of the hieroglyphic text being banned, the ability to read and write hieroglyphic text was lost, and not regained, for over 1,500 years. One of the great success stories of modern archaeology was the decipherment of the hieroglyphic script.

DISCOVERY OF THE 'KEY'

In 1798, Napoleon Bonaparte, with an army of soldiers and 151 scholars, conquered the Mamelukes, Ottoman rulers of Egypt, with the intention of colonising the country. He had taken the scholars with him so everything the French invaders saw and discovered could be recorded in words,

Figure 85 Napoleon Bonaparte

measurements and drawings. Ancient artefacts were logged and then stored for eventual transportation back to France, many of them destined to be displayed in the Louvre, Paris.

One year after arriving in Egypt a large slab of stone was discovered by Pierre Bouchard, one of Napoleon's soldiers, while he was digging the foundations of an addition to a fort near the town of el-Rashid (Rosetta), just east of the city of Alexandria. It was lying in the rubble and had been part of the foundations of a wall. The French scholars recognised its significance as it was in three different scripts but they could not decipher it; the stone was put in a storeroom with other antiquities, ready for shipment to France. However, the British army arrived in Egypt in 1801, defeated Napoleon and his army and the stone became British property under the terms of the Capitulation of Alexandria, together with those other antiquities that the French had not already sent to France. The Rosetta Stone, named after the town where it was found, is now in the British Museum. It has been continuously exhibited since its acquisition, except for two short instances. During the First World War it was relocated fifty feet below the ground in a disused tube tunnel near Holborn for safekeeping, and in 1972 it was loaned for a month to the Louvre for an exhibition.

It was originally a stele, a freestanding carved piece of stone that would have had a rounded top, probably decorated with a winged sun and images of gods. It is made from granodiorite, a hard, dark grey granite-like stone with a pink vein, quarried near Aswan in southern Egypt. It measures 112 cm in height, is 76 cm wide and 28 cm thick and weighs 762 kg. To commemorate it as 'war booty' it has a text on the left of the slab, stencilled in white paint 'CAPTURED IN EGYPT BY THE BRITISH ARMY IN 1801'. One year later the king presented it to the British Museum and this occasion is recorded on the right side; 'PRESENTED BY KING GEORGE III'. Both texts are now barely legible.

It does not look very impressive but this piece of stone was the key to deciphering the hieroglyphs.

The Stone records the text of a decree written in three scripts: Hieroglyphic, Demotic and Classical Greek, some of which is missing in all three languages. The broken upper part is covered with fourteen lines of hieroglyphs – it has been estimated that it was originally twenty-nine lines. Below this are thirty-two lines in ancient Demotic, and the bottom register has fifty-four lines

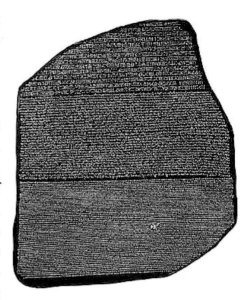

Figure 86 The Rosetta Stone

of Classical Greek text, the language of the administration in 196 BC, the time the decree was written.

Each block of script records the same judicial proclamation, known as the Memphis Decree, after its place of origin. It was issued by a synod of priests in Year 9 of Ptolemy V's reign. The priests were a very powerful section of society, second only to the pharaoh, and this decree is an expression of power and compromise between them. In it the priests promise to establish the divine cult of the pharaoh, meaning they would tell the people he was a god, he would be revered and have feast days in his honour. In exchange, the pharaoh promised them tax exemptions and gifts of precious materials such as gold and silver.

The Rosetta Stone's significance is that it became the key to unlocking the Egyptian hieroglyphic script, greatly advancing our understanding of ancient Egyptian history and culture.

WHO 'UNLOCKED' THE LANGUAGE?

The British took copies and engravings of the text and distributed them throughout Europe and America to all places of learning so that scholars could work on deciphering the text. After years of

study, there were two scholars who are credited with 'cracking the code' of the hieroglyphic script. The first was Thomas Young (1773-1829), an English doctor and internationally recognised polymath, a noted genius in varied disciplines, including wave theory of light.

Figure 87 Thomas Young

He succeeded in recognising many of the words in the decree in both demotic and hieroglyphics and was the first scholar to accurately identify groups of hieroglyphs. In 1816, he deciphered part of two cartouches containing the names of Ptolemy and Berenice by correctly identifying that the symbols represented letters of the alphabet. His big failing was that he incorrectly believed all the pictures simply represented letters of the alphabet.

Young did very well but the hero of the time was the French genius Jean François Champollion (1790-1832). From a young age, he had been excited by the idea of reading the Rosetta Stone and studied many languages in preparation for tackling the hieroglyphic script. He became very knowledgeable of Hebrew, Coptic, Arabic, Syriac, Chaldean, Sanskrit and Chinese.

Figure 88 Champollion

His breakthrough with hieroglyphics came in 1822, when he rightfully claimed success in his work. While Young had discovered parts of an alphabet, Champollion unlocked an entire written language. He realised that the hieroglyphic script was made up of pictograms that represented the thing they looked like, phonetic or alphabet signs that represent a sound, and determinatives that give meaning to the word.

From that day on, scholars have worked on deciphering scripts found on papyri, temple and tomb walls, scraps of pottery and beautiful funerary goods, in fact, anything that archaeologists have been able to find. The Ancient Egyptians' words have revealed to us a complex and sophisticated world of which nothing was previously known.

READING HIEROGLYPHS

Each symbol is referred to as a 'hieroglyph' but the language as a whole is called 'hieroglyphic script' or 'hieroglyphics'. More than 6,000 signs have been identified, the majority introduced during the Ptolemaic and Roman periods. Less than 1,000 signs existed during the Pharaonic period and there was a nucleus of about 700 signs that were in frequent use. The signs represent everything the Egyptians could see around them such as animals, birds, trees, buildings etc.

There are three different types of signs:

Pictograms: picture signs, symbols that represent what they look like e.g. face, eye, mouth, with a line underneath (a pictogram indicator) e.g.

I a face

Phonograms: sound signs of 1, 2 or 3 consonants. The 1 consonant signs are also called 'alphabet' signs (see table on page 141). Examples of phonograms:

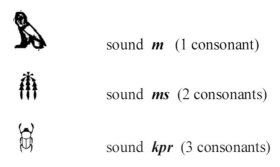

sound ***m*** (1 consonant)

sound ***ms*** (2 consonants)

sound ***kpr*** (3 consonants)

Determinatives: symbols that are placed at the end of a group of hieroglyphs to help us know the meaning of the previous sound signs. They do not have a sound value. Here is an example:

this is the symbol for 'man' and is a determinative for words relating to man's relationships and occupations e.g. son, brother, scribe or farmer. It is also used following a man's personal name. The following group of hieroglyphs meaning 'servant' has a 2 consonant phonogram sign giving the sound *'ba'* followed by a 1 consonant sign that gives the sound *'k'*; together they spell *bak* (servant) and we are clear about its meaning because the word is followed by a 'man' determinative.

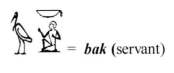

= **bak** (servant)

ba   k

In English, the same spelling for a word can have more than one meaning, e.g. crop can mean 'to cut' or it can refer to the harvest brought in by a farmer, and crook can either be a criminal or a shepherd's staff. The same applies to hieroglyphics, but having a determinative clarifies for the reader the exact intended meaning of the word; in English we have to read the word in context with the rest of the sentence to understand the writer's meaning.

Like other languages, Ancient Egyptian was quite complex with complicated rules of grammar governing its structure of nouns, verbs, adjectives etc. To get started:

FIVE SIMPLE TIPS:

1. There are no spaces between words and no punctuation: butyoucanreadthiseasilybecauseyoucanreadenglish

2. It can be read in any direction, but usually right to left ◄ or top to bottom ▼. The symbols are often grouped (not in a straight line) to save space or to look more pleasing to the eye.

3. The faces of people/things are always looking at the beginning of the text.

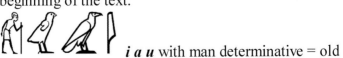

i a u with man determinative = old

u   a   i

138

4. There are insufficient vowels for us to speak it correctly in English, so insert 'imaginary' vowels where necessary.

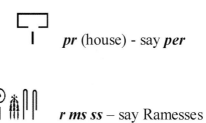

pr (house) - say *per*

r ms ss – say Ramesses

5. The names of pharaohs are always enclosed within a cartouche, and no other words are treated in this way (the word 'cartouche' is a French term describing the bullet-shaped form of the knotted rope). Seeing

Neb-kheperu-re

them within the hieroglyphic text on the Rosetta Stone gave Thomas Young the idea that the symbols inside must be 'something special'- he was right! The line enclosing the pharaoh's name represents a length of knotted rope that symbolised 'encircling protection' around the king's name. The protection given to the name magically ensured that the body of the pharaoh, whether alive or in its mummified form, was also protected for eternity. This cartouche encloses the name Nebkheperure, the throne name of the young Pharaoh Tutankhamun.

Numbers:

The Ancient Egyptians had a relatively simple numbering structure, it being a base 10 system the same as used in the UK.

1 = 𓏤   10 = 𓎆   100 = 𓍢   1,000 = 𓆼

10,000 = 𓂭   100,000 = 𓆐

therefore, reading from left to right:

𓆼 𓆼 𓍢 𓎆   𓎆 𓏤 𓏤 𓏤 = 2,123

You can now read and write numbers in

Ancient Egypt's sacred language!

Personal names were written using phonograms, mainly the 1 consonant (alphabet) signs or 2 consonant signs. Here are two British names translated into hieroglyphs:

Simon: with a 'man' determinative for a male name. It would be spelt the same for the female version Simone, with a 'female' determinative.

Chris: with a 'female' determinative.

The following page has the alphabet signs.

Try spelling your own name!

Table 1

The one-consonant or "alphabet" signs, with sound value					
Symbol	Sound	Symbol	Sound	Symbol	Sound
vulture	ah	water	n	basket	k
reed	i/a	mouth	r	jar stand	g
two reeds	y	shelter	h	loaf	t
forearm	ah	flex	h (gutteral)	tethering rope	tj
quail chick	w / u	placenta	kh ("loch")	hand	d
foot	b	animal's belly	kh (German "ich")	snake	j
stool	p	bolt or folded cloth	s	pool	sh
horned viper	f	hill / slope	k	owl	m

141

13   PARTY TIME

Celebrations with Fun for All

Scholars of Ancient Egypt tend to concentrate on the Egyptians' seeming obsession with gods, death and the Afterlife, but they loved life and lived it to the full. They knew how to party and celebrated whenever they could but records are scarce, limited to a few written stories and painted scenes in tombs.

There are no records of birthdays being celebrated, but a work record from Deir el-Medina stated that a man was absent because it was 'his festival day' which possibly meant his birthday and he had taken the day off to celebrate with family and friends.

There are no records of wedding ceremonies and there does not seem to have been a requirement to have a couple's union confirmed, either legally or religiously. It is apparent that a couple could set up home together without any official involvement. There is one recorded wedding celebration (*the Story of Setne*) and that was in the Greco-Roman period, after the end of the period we call Ancient Egypt. It was a grand affair as the bride was a princess; it records gifts of silver and gold from the pharaoh and the fact that the groom entertained the entire court before taking his new wife to bed. Earlier Egyptians probably celebrated in similar fashion but we cannot say for sure.

What we do know is that they celebrated religious festivals. In Britain we celebrate festivals such as Christmas, Passover, Diwali and Eid al-Hada with good food, drink, music and dancing, and the Ancient Egyptians did exactly the same!

They had more than sixty religious festivals throughout the year, some lasting a day but others went on for more than a week. Each village and town had many local festivals linked to their particular deities, but there were also important national events such as the New Year Festival and the Festival of Opet. Each event was typified by a procession in which an image/statue of a god was carried from one temple to another.

A typical annual festival was the Beautiful Festival of the Valley

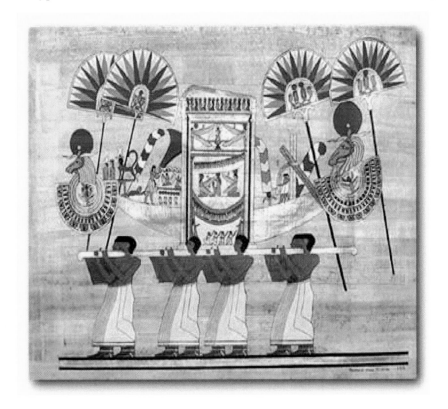

Figure 89 Opet Festival

which was held at Thebes (Karnak) from the early 18th Dynasty onwards. Statues of the Theban triad (3 related gods) Amun, Mut and their son, the moon-god Khons, were carried in procession from

Karnak, across the Nile to the West Bank, and on to the Temple of Hathor at Deir el-Bahri and back again.

Local dignitaries, the elite of society and priests, would be part of the procession while the common people lined the route. They took this opportunity to consult the oracle about their personal concerns and receive an answer from the god. The questions had to be direct, and capable of having a 'yes' or 'no' answer. If the answer from the god was 'yes', the platform on which he was being carried tipped forward; if the answer was 'no' it tipped backwards – the people were satisfied that their god had spoken!

The officials enjoyed banquets at the sites of the temples and the people not involved in the procession made merry with a festival outside the tombs of their relatives or at home.

For anyone going to a party, the first thing to do is to get dressed up, and the Egyptians were no exception! Like us, they had make-up, fancy hairstyles, and 'best' clothes…let us take a look:

COSMETICS

This cosmetic box belonged to Merit, wife of Kha, the overseer of works from Deir el-Medina in the mid-18th Dynasty, and was found in their tomb. It is a brightly painted wooden box and contained beautiful jars made from alabaster and glass. They contained everything Merit needed to make herself beautiful

Figure 90 Merit's Beauty Box

for a party:

Moisturiser Moringa oil was particularly good and did not go rancid very easily. The leaves are edible but the oil from its seeds is very special and was used as a moisturiser. A jar of it, still sweet and usable, was found in an 18th Dynasty tomb of Maya, an official at Memphis.

Eye make-up Black kohl, made from grinding galena (lead sulphide) mixed with water, was used as cosmetic eyeliner by men and women, and was worn by children during the day since it reduced the glare from the sun. It was applied with a fine stick or brush. As well as looking very attractive, they believed that this style of eyeliner also had magical, protective qualities. It symbolised the Eye of Horus, the eye of the falcon god that represented healing and resurrection.

A popular eye shadow was green malachite (which is a copper-based mineral), often put along the lower eyelid for special occasions.

Blusher/Lipstick Ochre ranging in colours from pale yellow, through orange to deep red was readily available, lying loose upon the ground. The women ground it, mixed it with oil or water and used it as blusher and lipstick to bring some colour into their faces.

DRESS

Once they were made up, the next step for the ladies (and men) was to choose a nice outfit for the evening. For every-day wear, everyone except royalty and the elite wore very simple shift dresses of varying lengths made from heavy-duty linen. However, for a party they had the very finest linen, sometimes pleated and trimmed

Figure 92 Dressed for a Party

with beads, and beautifully diaphanous. Of course, the more affluent the partygoers, the better quality their material.

They were usually bare-foot but sometimes wore sandals made from woven papyrus plants or leather trimmed with precious materials if they were wealthy.

Figure 91 Typical Sandals

JEWELLERY

Now the party-goers were dressed they would adorn themselves in their favourite pieces of jewellery. In practically all banqueting scenes, both men and women are wearing colourful, wide collars made from precious materials such as gold, lapis lazuli and carnelian or more affordable materials such as faience. This

Figure 93 Gold Collar

one is a replica of an ancient collar, which was made from gold and lapis lazuli beads representing flies, believed to bestow resilience and perseverance on the wearer.

As well as a bead collar, the women would have worn plain hoop earrings and a few bangles. The best of the bracelets were in gold and silver and decorated with animals and amulets: there might be a snake gripping a turtle by the neck, several *wedjat*-eyes, running hares, hawks, *ankhs* and headless serpents, to name a few. The bracelets looked very attractive and the women who wore them believed they protected them against demons, and gave them health and long life. They are very similar to the charm bracelets worn by some women today to help bring good luck.

HAIR/WIGS

Last but not least, everyone did their hair. Both men and women wore wigs for banquets and parties; the ladies wore them past their shoulders and the men had a shorter style. Long hair was seen to be

youthful and therefore desirable but for practical purposes, most people had very short hair. It was cooler in the very high temperatures of the summer months and reduced the chance of catching head lice.

The majority of wigs were made from human hair but a few have been found made from vegetable material. They also had hair extensions that were either braided or tied into their own hair to lengthen and thicken it, much the same as we do today.

Figure 94 Wigs & Oil Cones

On top of their wig, according to scenes such as this, they wore a cone shaped decoration, thought to be of solid scented oil. As the evening progressed, the oil melted and filled the room with its perfume, which is quite a nice idea, except for the oil dripping through the wig and onto their best clothes! Some say the cones were symbolic and represented the fact that the wearers had scented themselves with perfume.

The Ancient Egyptians were famous for their beautiful perfume. The distillation process favoured by the great French perfumers had not yet been discovered but the Egyptians used an oil base that kept the perfume smelling fresh and new for many years, just like the best perfumes we have today. A jar of perfume was found in the tomb of Tutankhamun – still fresh and fragrant!

GIFTS

When we go to a celebration at someone's house nowadays, we usually take a small gift as a token of our gratitude – the Ancient Egyptians did the same. It is common practice for people today to take the party hosts a small gift of wine, beer, flowers and chocolates, or a combination of all of them. In Ancient Egypt, they took bread, beer and cakes which would have been a contribution to the feast, otherwise unaffordable by the host. Found at Deir el-Medina, here is part of a list recorded by the hostess, of gifts brought to her party by twenty guests. One assumes it was so the hostess could reciprocate in correct fashion when she was invited to their home for a party.

Wabet, daughter of Ipuy *– 10 cakes*

2 bundles of vegetables

1 jar of beer

FOOD

The daily diet of non-elite Ancient Egyptians were the staple foods of bread and beer, supplemented by vegetables, pulses and fish. For special celebrations they would have the best they could afford which would include a real treat for them – meat!

MEAT
The more affluent people of society would eat meat quite regularly and beef seems to have been their favourite, but it was a rare delicacy for the poor. The Egyptians drank cow's milk but it soon turned sour in the heat, so most of it was made into yoghurt and cheese.

The Egyptians also raised chickens (for meat and eggs), pigs and goats, and hunted for wild hares and small deer. There is evidence that they used the forced feeding method, called

Figure 95 Herd of Cows

gavage, to fatten up geese quickly; they had noticed that geese ate large amounts of food during the winter months, prior to their migratory flight, which fattened the liver. Today we call it foie-gras - a delicacy and treat for Ancient Egyptian banquets.

FISH

The Nile was absolutely teeming with lots of different edible fish

such as tilapia, perch, eels and catfish. The fish were cleaned and the eggs set apart for further treatment while the flesh was eaten roasted, boiled, pickled in brine or dried in the sun. It

Figure 96 Catching Fish

would definitely have been on the menu of any banquet.

BREAD

Bread was made from emmer wheat, which is similar to spelt. It is a hulled wheat which is quite labour-intensive since it needs more pounding than common wheat to break off the husks to leave the flour. They made it in all shapes and sizes, usually round and flat for everyday eating, but they also made it using different shaped moulds for special occasions.

It was unleavened i.e. they did not use yeast, just mixed it with salt and water for normal use and flavoured it with spices such as cumin seeds, fruit (dates) or honey for special occasions. For those who could afford it there was also fine bread and cakes baked from high-grade flour.

VEGETABLES

Vegetables and pulses were an important part of their daily diet, including lettuce, onions, lentils and chickpeas. They also grew garlic, radishes, celery and cucumber together with leeks and cabbages; quite a selection and the basis of a good diet. Mixed with a wide range of spices including cumin, coriander, anise and marjoram, their food would have been tasty as well as healthy.

DESSERT

No party food is complete without a delicious dessert to finish the meal, and the usual 'sweet' was fruit, sometimes served with small cakes or drizzled with honey. The fruit that was available to them included dates, figs, pomegranates, grapes, watermelons and dom-palm nuts.

They also had carob from the powdered pods of the St John's Locust tree, often used now as a substitute for cocoa powder, so sufficient on the party table to satisfy anyone's sweet tooth!

DRINK

What did they drink at the party? Like a lot of us, they enjoyed beer and wine, and sometimes drank too much!

BEER

The water in Egypt was unsafe to drink, so everyone including children drank beer. It was thicker and more nourishing than the beer we drink today, more like a soup. It was made from the previous day's stale bread, with water and barley added and then left to ferment. It was often flavoured with dates or other fruit and was thought to have had alcohol content similar to the beers we drink today.

WINE

There is evidence that the Egyptians made and drank red wine and possibly had white wine too. Of twenty-six wine amphorae found in Tutankhamun's tomb, chemical testing indicates that one amphora had contained white wine, the rest had contained red. In Figure 97 several men are trampling grapes underfoot to extract the juice, and

the amphorae are standing on a shelf ready to be filled.

There were different qualities of wine; some were from a single grape variety and others were 'blended', using different varieties of grapes together. Some were flavoured with fruit, usually dates and spices. They made the wine in a very similar

Figure 97 Men Pressing grapes

way to modern methods and even labelled the jars with the name of the vineyard and the year of production. The amphorae of wine held all the details, either written into the shoulder or impressed onto the mud seals.

It has been suggested that the revellers also nibbled on lotus petals or dropped them into their drinks (rather than sniffing them as shown in most banqueting scenes). The lotus flower, when mixed with alcohol, has a narcotic effect, is slightly hallucinogenic and is also a gentle aphrodisiac.

Sometimes they drank too much and there are plenty of records of villagers getting into trouble for behaving badly while drunk. In a famous text, The *Instruction of Ani,* (18th Dynasty) a father warns his son *"Don't indulge in drinking beer, because something bad will come out of your mouth. You won't know what you are saying".* A fair warning to us all!

However, like parties these days, often an indication of a good one is how much alcohol is available and how much

Figure 98 Vomiting Scene

everyone drinks; being drunk was a sign that everyone had a good time. Unfortunately, a few of them will have ended the evening like this, vomiting. This scene is depicted in a few tombs so it is thought to have been quite a common occurrence.

Fortunately, they did have several cures for a hangover. One prescription advises taking chopped onions and mixing them with salt, oil and several types of fish; crayfish, bones of swordfish skull and redfish. When it was all mixed together, relief came after leaving it smeared on the head for four days.

ENTERTAINMENT

MUSICIANS

This is a group of female musicians with various instruments, preparing to make the party go with a swing.

The woman on the left has a harp while her neighbour is holding a lute. In the centre is a young girl, probably a dancer and the two other musicians are carrying a double flute and another type of harp.

Figure 100 Group of Musicians

They are all beautifully dressed but in different styles, ranging from the semi-naked woman and young girl who are wearing just a girdle around their hips, to the others who are wearing fine linen dresses which are embroidered and pleated, and

Figure 99 Sistrum

in one case, delicately diaphanous. We know exactly what each individual instrument sounded like as many have been found in tombs and are not dissimilar to modern instruments. I imagine that when they were played together the music would have been very similar to Egyptian music today.

A blind male harpist, hand clapping, a drum and a sistrum that was held in the hand and shaken, to give a rattly, tinkly sound, often accompanied the chief musicians. The sistrum was played primarily by women during

154

rituals and religious ceremonies and is particularly associated with the goddess Hathor.

DANCERS

Guests at a banquet were also entertained by dancing girls and acrobats as shown here, (can you spot the artist's error?) Dancing appears to have been a very important activity associated with rituals and celebrations as well as funerary ceremonies and always accompanied

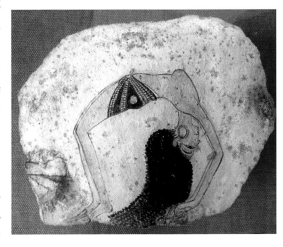

Figure 101 Acrobat

by music. Men and women are never shown dancing together; the most common scenes are of women dancing, often in pairs.

(The artist's error: the hoop earring would naturally hang downwards; this one apparently defied gravity!).

PARTY GAMES

For those who wanted a quieter party, the Ancient Egyptians' most popular board game was *senet*. It was for two players, each with seven pieces distinguished by shape or colour, and they played on a

Figure 102 Senet Board Game

grid of thirty squares that were arranged in three rows of ten. The rules of the game have been lost but it is thought that the idea of the game was to get your pieces around the snaking track before your opponent, via a number of squares representing good or bad fortune.

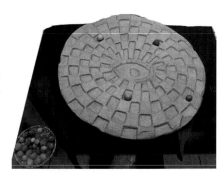

Figure 103 The Snake Game

Another popular game was *mehen,* the snake game. A limestone board, carved in the shape of a coiled serpent, was used by two teams of up to six players to race marbles around the snake from tail to head and back again. Victory in this game, as well as being fun, was meant to symbolise success in the Afterlife.

Whatever a party-goers' idea of a good time was, the celebrations and banquets of Ancient Egypt provided a good choice of entertainment, something for everyone.

.

14   APPENDIX

LIST OF FIGURES

GLOSSARY OF TERMS

akh spirit of the dead enduring for eternity.

ankh hieroglyphic symbol for life, traditionally carried by gods and royalty.

ba the essence of a dead person's personality, often represented by the deceased's head on a hawk's body.

deben unit of weight of 91 grams.

ka the life force of an individual, present throughout their life, and represented as their 'twin'.

Book of the Dead the modern name for the 'Book of Going Forth by Day', a selection of illustrated spells to guide the dead through the Underworld.

cartouche an oval shaped ouline representing a length of knotted rope which contained royal titles. It signified the concept of 'encircling protection' for eternity.

hypostyle hall large court within a temple filled with columns of varying diameter and height, representing a reed swamp at the beginning of creation.

inundation annual flooding of the Nile in Egypt

lector priest literally 'he who carries the ritual book'; a priest who recited ritual texts during funerals and at temple ceremonies.

natron a natural salt mainly containing sodium carbonate decahydrate (hydrated soda ash), from the Wadi el Natrun in the Egyptian Delta. Used for cooking, drying food and mummification.

nilometer device for measuring the height of the Nile

nome one of 42 administrative districts, each of which had its own god.

nomarch governor of one of the 42 administrative districts

ostraca potsherd or flake of limestone used as a writing surface, ranging in size from a few centimetres to over a metre long.

shabti funerary figure intended to serve the deceased in the Afterlife.

uraeus the royal cobra displayed on the forehead or crown. It was believed to spit fire at the king's enemies.

vizier chief administrative officer (Prime Minister).

wedjat-**eye** protective symbol representing the eye of Horus.

wisdom texts genre of 'instruction' texts offering a series of maxims on the way to live correctly; the Instructions of Any being one of the most popular. It is from an older man to his son and comments on religion, motherhood, honesty, restraint and the avoidance of relations with unfaithful women.

SUGGESTED FURTHER READING

For readers interested in learning more about specific topics, I can recommend the following books:

Bierbrier, M. 2003 *The Tomb-Builders of the Pharaohs* London BMP

Collier, M. & Manley, B. *How to Read Egyptian Hieroglyphs* 2000 BMP

Manley, Bill 1996 *The Penguin Historical Atlas of Ancient Egypt* London Penguin Books

McDowell, A.G. 2001 *Village Life in Ancient Egypt Laundry Lists and Love Songs* Oxford OUP

Lehner, M. 2008 *The Complete Pyramids* London Thames & Hudson

Pinch, Geraldine 1974 *Magic in Ancient Egypt* London BMP

Robins, Gay 1998 *Women in Ancient Egypt* London BMP

ACKNOWLEDGEMENTS

Figure numbers in bold.

Front Cover: Pyramids at Giza hurst-ancienthistory-kis.wikispaces.com
35 adolescentlitandmyth.wikispaces.com **5** Rymer
Eric,ancienttravelerjournal.wikispaces.com **68** ant3145-nilevalleygods.wikispaces.com **48**
84 bowersarthistory.wikispaces.com **102** carnet-aux-petites-choses.fr **19** claseshistoria.com
13 17 28 55 56 95 100 cowofgold.wikispaces.com **67** cynical-c.com **72 75 98**
dianabuja.wordpress.com **32 53** E. Goulding **8** egyptiangoddesses.wikispaces.com **57**
egyptologyatperk.wikispaces.com **9 16 54** eng12mythwiki12.wikispaces.com **22** Jeff
Dahl,es.wikipedia.org **41** AtonX, es.wikipedia.org **47 49 59** es.wikipedia.org **80** John
campana,es.wikipedia.org **76** studyblue,es.wikipedia.org **99**
evolutionofmusic.wikispaces.com **7** Maureen Amerune,flickr.com **45**
Kamenatenla.sk,flickr.com **60** David Berkowitz, flickr.com **6** ArianZwegers,flickr.com **78**
redes-cepalcala.org **81** andreapravettoni, famouswonders.com **90** J.P.Dalbera,flickr.com **93**
jankunst, flickr.com**74 90** flickr.com **34** foxstox.deviantart.com **15 24** Jeff
Dahl,fr.wikipedia.org **23** goldenmeadows en.wikipedia **37** Keith Schengili-
Roberts,fr.wikipedai.org **63** Althiphika, fr.wikipedia.org **65**
messerwoland,fr.wikipedia.org**12** Jon Bodsworth, fr.wikipedia.org **82** marcus
cyron,fr.wikipedia.org **25 88** fr.wikipedia.org **6** geolocation.ws **31** guity-
novin.blogspot.com **39** historyohya.wikispaces.com **62** hurst-ancienthistory-
kis.wikispaces.com **1 4 10 27 30 64 83 94 101 103** G. Goulding **33**
goldengoblet.wikispaces.com **86** gravesenglishclass.wikispaces.com **2**
gretchennorland.wikispaces.com **87** il-trafiletto.blogspot.it **77** imperial-
egyptianart.wikispaces.com **70 96** jhayesteach.wikispaces.com **91**
johnstone6.wikispaces.com **43** maple-green-division-3.wikispaces.com
11RobertMeyergloss18,masonic.wikidot.com **42** mystic-lotus.blogspot.com **26**
mythprojects.wikispaces.com **51** nefertiti.wikispaces.com **52** tataryn77, ookaboo.com **18**
oudheid.wikispaces.com **46** pedro-mundodebabel.blogspot.com **79**
period60910.wikispaces.com **40** pharaohsofancientegypt6201.wikispaces.com **85**
purotip.com **92** rlasharespace2012.wikispaces.com **38**
resourcesforhistoryteachers.wikispaces.com **58** sghshistoryofmedicine.wikispaces.com
50suurmiehet.wikispaces.com **14** thegrandstones.wikidot.com **44** the-norwood-
globe.wikispaces.com **29** tigger5.wikispaces.com **3 97** ucfant3145f09-04.wikispaces.com
89 vico.wikispaces.com **73** visual-language.wikispaces.com **69**whitelocust.wordpress.com
66 cary bass-deschenes,wondermondo.com **21** whydoyoueatthat.wordpress.com **72**
www.chem.uwimona.edu.jm **20** ya-ancientegypt.wikispaces.com **36**
5thperiodegypt.wikispaces.com

*All website figures sourced under 'free to share and use commercially' licence bing.com/images 18th
and 19th October 2014*

INDEX